PRAISES

"If life is a journey, as some say, flying through life must be the ultimate way to go. The veteran pilot author of this helpful volume writes from knowledge in both the art of aviation and the craft of successful living. Read and enjoy the excitement and adventure, the challenges and uncertainties of living on the edge. Your faith will be stretched and affirmed, and your mind will be acclimated to new ways of thinking about your own spiritual journey."

—Dr. Loren Gresham, President,
Southern Nazarene University

"The author paints incredible word pictures, reminding us to use all available resources to find the best path through impending life pitfalls; then depend on God to lead us through the narrow passages to safety."

—Rev. Henry Cheatham,
Retired Pastor

"I have flown at 35,000 feet countless times and places with the airlines. I'd rather be in a shaking plane with a steady captain than a steady plane with a shaking captain. Here are stories about airline flying, written by my friend Renda, a calm United Airlines pilot with Christ as captain of his life."

—Charles R. Millhuff, D.Min. Evangelist, Editor
Evangelist Perspective Magazine

L I F E
AT 35,000 FEET

Defying Gravity, A Spiritual Perspective

ISBN-13: 978-0692996799

RENDA BRUMBELOE

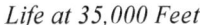

Life at 35,000 Feet
Copyright © 2010 by Captain Renda Brumbeloe. All rights reserved.

No part of this publication may be reproduced, stored in a retrieval system or transmitted in any way by any means, electronic, mechanical, photocopy, recording or otherwise without the prior permission of the author except as provided by USA copyright law.

Scripture quotations marked (niv) are taken from the Holy Bible, New International Version®. niv®. Copyright© 1973, 1978, 1984 by International Bible Society. Used by permission of Zondervan. All rights reserved.
Scripture quotations marked (nkjv) are taken from the New King James Version®.
Copyright © 1982 by Thomas Nelson, Inc. Used by permission. All rights reserved Scripture quotations marked (kjv) are taken from the Holy Bible, King James Version, Cambridge, 1769. Used by permission. All rights reserved.
Scripture quotations marked (nasb) are taken from the New American Standard Bible® copyright © 1960, 1962, 1963, 1968, 1971, 1972, 1973, 1975, 1977, 1995 by The Lockman Foundation. Used by permission.
Scripture quotations marked (nlt) are taken from the Holy Bible, New Living Translation, copyright © 1996. Used by permission of Tyndale House Publishers, Inc., Wheaton, Illinois 60189. All rights reserved.
Scripture quotations marked (tniv) are taken from the Holy Bible, Today's New International Version ®. tniv®. Copyright© 2001, 2005 by International Bible Society. Used by permission of Zondervan. All rights reserved.
Scripture quotations marked (msg) are taken from The Message. Copyright © 1993, 1994, 1995, 1996, 2000, 2001, 2002. Used by permission of NavPress Publishing Group.
Scripture quotations marked (ncv) are taken from the New Century Version®. Copyright © 2005 by Th omas Nelson, Inc. Used by permission. All rights reserved.
Scripture quotations marked (hcsb) are taken from the Holman Christian Standard Bible®, Copyright © 1999, 2000, 2002, 2003 by Holman Bible Publishers. Used by permission. Holman Christian Standard Bible®, Holman CSB®, and HCSB® are federally registered trademarks of Holman Bible Publishers.

Second Printing 2018
Published in the United States of America
ISBN: 978-0692996799
Cover by Scott Soliz ZealDesino.com
Published by Allsbury.com

1. Religion, Christian Life, Devotional
2. Religion, Christian Life, Spiritual Growth
10.08.11

DEDICATION

IT IS WITH GREAT LOVE and gratitude for my mom and dad, Thelma and Barney Brumbeloe, that I write this manuscript. They gave me my first wings to fly. I dedicate this book to their unending love and memory.

My mother taught me the importance of patience and quiet persistence. Moreover, her demonstration and good humor dispelled my fears when I doubted myself.

My dad taught me not to wait for a plan to drop into my lap. Start the job now. The plan will come as you begin the work.

He constantly reminded me of how proud he was of me. Repeatedly, he reminded me that I could do or be anything I wanted to do or be. He would say, "Son, you have the will, the brains, and the drive to do it."

My parents gave me my wings to fly and "soloed" me at the perfect time.

ACKNOWLEDGMENTS

I AM HONORED TO HAVE special friends that I have known since my youth. Among this group, there are two who are more than boyhood chums I grew up with in Alabama. They have become close spiritual friends to whom I can express myself.

One is my dear friend Stuart McWhirter, who has urged me to commit my stories to print. I have not taken his encouragement lightly, for he is a master of the English language and a wordsmith of highest accomplishment. It has served him well, for he has preached around the world in churches, notable camp meetings, and religious conferences. Stuart's sermons and written words inspirationally capture for me the essence of biblical history and Christian message. Our childhood and upbringing are parallel. We are phone friends and have shared our ideas, our writing, and convictions deeply and often. He always leaves me in a literary buzz.

Another is a teenage friend from my hometown, Jesse Middendorf. We both were preacher's kids and shared unspoken semblance in our lifestyles. I correctly predicted when he was seventeen that he would eventually be elected to the office of general superintendent in the International Church of the Nazarene. Jesse, who also is a private pilot, upon reading my flying stories, strongly encouraged me to pursue publishing them for their flying interest and spiritual analogy.

I am thankful for my dear friends: for Lyle and Johann Parker, my comrades in life, missionaries and pastors, whose encouraging friendship has enlarged my thoughts and creatively spurred my thinking as I have written this manuscript; and for Dr. Tom Barnard, my dear friend, educator, teacher, and senior encourager, for his spiritual insights; and to my late friend Dr.

Ponder Gilliland, my senior pastor who mentored me in shared ministry.

Becoming a writer takes years of reading, scribbling, note taking, and idea processing. I cannot read a book without pencil in hand to scribble in the margins my thoughts and reactions to the author's ideas and presentation. I am thankful to live in a family of readers and skilled linguists who have encouraged me.

Finally, to my wife, Sharon, I give the most gratitude for always encouraging me to put feet under my dreams. She has listened, read, edited, and suggested ideas to improve my writing process.

FOR DISCUSSION GROUPS

The Table of Contents Of **"Life at 35,000 Feet"** is divided into a vocational flow of four parts.

    Part One - A Definitive Beginning,

    Part Two – Flight School with God,

    Part Three-- Making Adjustments,

    Part Four – The Advanced Journey

These airline stories work very well into all our different vocations. However, if desired, they do not necessarily have to be read in book order from front to back.
The motif is that the flight crew, the passengers, and the airplane as well, are all on a journey, each with undefined but sure destinations. The stories in the book reveal how God's Word interfaces with our lives, whatever our particular vocation and life experiences. This alone can make for vibrant discussion.

Table of Contents

For Discussion Groups..............................11
Forward................................... 16
Preface..18

PART ONE

A Definitive Beginning............................27
The Authority of God's Word......................29
Back to Basics....................................31
Climbing Like a Homesick Angel...................33
Longing..35
The Gooneybird Experience........................37
Merely Keeping the Rules.........................40
Flying by the Seat of Your Pants.................42
Discernment......................................43
The Flight Plan..................................46
Flight Canceled..................................48
Let us Lay Aside Every Weight....................51
Indecision.......................................53
Are You a Fundamentalist?........................56
No Cock and Bull.................................58
Strapping on the Yoke............................60
The Greatest Moments.............................62
Perseverance.....................................64
Pilot Fatigue....................................66
Empty Airplanes..................................68
Air Traffic Control Communication................70

False Radio Communications......................72
Middle "C"..74
Core Beliefs..76
The Main Things....................................78
Disqualified..81
What does the Book Say?............................83
The Black Box......................................85

PART TWO

Flight School with God.............................87
Becoming an Experienced Pilot......................90
The Autopilot......................................93
For the Love of Flying.............................95
Away from Home and Commuting.......................98
Weeds...101
Finding the Pearl of Great Price..................102
The Flight Deck...................................103
The Glide Scope...................................105
Holy Days...107
The Touchdown Zone................................108
Who do you Trust?.................................111
The Glorious Grace of the Good News...............114
Hazmat in the Christian Life......................116
Near Misses.......................................118
The Lord is my Rock...............................120
Museum Relics.....................................122
Where are We?.....................................124
A Flight Delay....................................126
The Center Line...................................128
My Brother's Keeper...............................131

Chain of Events..................................132
God's Higher Plane............................134
The Need for High Flight......................135
Agendas and Hoaxes..........................137

PART THREE

Making Adjustments............................140
Abruptness.......................................142
So How do You Fly an Airplane?..........144
Help for the Journey............................145
The School Answer.............................147
Going Through the Motions...................150
Flirting with the Runway........................153
Consensus or Checklists......................155
Flying by Faith...................................157
Communications................................159
Deferred, Broken or Shattered...............160
Judging What Really Matters.................162
Icing at Low Altitudes...........................165
Silence the Warning Horn.....................167
Dumping Fuel....................................170
As Is..171
The Standard is One Hundred Percent....173
Our Righteousness..............................175
The Unknown Quadrant........................178
The Flight Recorder.............................180
Weight and Balance............................182
When Things Get Bent.........................184

PART FOUR

The Advanced Journey............................187
A Certain Word......................................189
The Importance of Taxiing........................191
The Nerve Center of Faith........................193
Knowledge Dedicated to a Smaller Framework.....195
Ambiguity on the Flight Deck......................199
Brush With 9/11....................................201
Ambiguity Unchecked..............................206
Faith in Action......................................209
Spiritual Maintenance.............................212
The Narrow Gate....................................214
The Flight Operating Manual......................216
Making Room for God..............................219
The Holy Spirit.....................................222
Where was the Power?............................224
Contaminated Fuel................................226
The Return Flight Home..........................228
Don't Worry...230
Don't Miss God's Glory...........................232
Holiday Flying......................................234
Believing in the word of God....................236

EPILOGUE

The Story..239
Finally Home.......................................241
My Eternal King....................................242
High Flight..243
Study & Discussion Guide........................245

FORWORD

THERE ARE SEVERAL THINGS MANY readers look for when choosing to spend some concentrated time with a book. One would certainly be whether or not the content of the book had appeal to their personal interests. It would be difficult for me, for example, to dig into a book on advanced calculus, as my inclinations are simply not in that direction. Another variable in selecting material for serious reading would be the applicability the material has to real life and living. Since science fiction has not been one of my interests, it may be unfair to assume that all readers desire something that relates to the daily realities of life.

For me, though, my time reading needs to find applicability to what my life challenges are.

A final thought in reader selection is that the content will have the chance of opening up some new avenues on how to think about my life and work. If there's little or no way that new perspectives emerge from the effort, time can be spent better in other activities.

From each of these angles, Captain Brumbeloe's volume fulfills the prerequisites of valuable time spent with a book. Even if the reader has no background in the theory of flight, the terminology of the cockpit, or the variables which meteorology can bring into an aircraft's trajectory, the reader can gain valuable life lessons from the content.

Beyond the interesting stories and information shared is the spiritual application the author makes to life. The flight lessons are of interest to me as a private pilot taught by the author, but those in and of themselves might not capture the occasional commercial traveler. However, the Christ follower can't help but take wonderful lessons with her from a reading of Life at 35,000 Feet. The spiritual journey is paired in creative ways to the earthly lessons gleaned from the experienced pilot with the pen. Often our lives are compared to a physical journey. We understand the metaphor of going from home to someplace distant or the return from such. It's an easy leap from that thought to the life journey which culminates in physical demise. For anyone who loves to travel, this book will be both enjoyable and challenging. For the Christian on the path to heaven, this book will make the images that may have been portrayed by ministers through sermons even more meaningful. For any person who wants to be what God has in mind for them to become, this volume will provide valuable lessons to make the progression through the years more interesting and comprehensible. I wish you the best on the airwaves as you read the captain's admonitions for the journey.

—Loren P. Gresham, PhD,
President, Southern Nazarene University

PREFACE

LITTLE DID I KNOW WHAT awaited me as I prepared myself for an airline career. Airline deregulation in 1978 produced turbulent ebb and flow in air travel for more than two decades. Later, my career would be influenced by the catastrophic event of 9/11. I would have a close encounter—and my own brush with 9/11—the story which I will relate later in this book.

Let's face it. Flying (defying gravity) is inherently dangerous. You never know what fate might await you. It's a lot like living, you might say. However, living and flying are made safer by the basic precautions and training to which we commit ourselves.

The intent of this book is not biographical. My life is no different from any other child who was born into a home of young Southern parents that lived a modest and frugal lifestyle, trying to make ends meet each week. They were like all their friends, taking life one day at a time, existing at the mercy of a textile town, doing shift work at the cotton mill.

Your first job in the mill was the spinning room. It was a demanding apprentice opportunity. The first sign of personal success was either being promoted to a job outside of the spinning room or leaving the cotton mill altogether. However, the latter would require vacating mill housing and finding more expensive living quarters. Real success, although viewed with suspect, was to leave the area and move into another economic system.

However, the Chattahoochee Valley was a happy place. It was my roots. The string of towns each had a cotton mill along the river. Each town sported a ballpark, and the lights were on every night of the year when the weather was mild. Every town had a community center where town meetings, festivals, and family parties continuously occurred. People knew and trusted each other. They lived with a unity of thought. The mills supplied a social life. Labor unions had no chance of gaining a foothold.

My dad, handsome and energetic, escaped the textile economy and became the top salesman for the Skinner Furniture Company. One day Reverend James Hamilton, a minister, knocked on our door and said to my dad, "You are young and have great potential, but you need God in your life. With a growing family, you need to get them into church."

My dad was convicted almost immediately and soon dedicated his life to God and the service of ministry. His conversion would be the event that forever changed our lives. My twin sister and I came into this world of uncertainty when my parents were exercising great faith, as they began preparing for a ministry that was yet to be revealed to them. Yes, I would be a preacher's kid.

Renda, age 6 – top left

I was born a musician, apparently with a proclivity of perfect pitch, but for sure, perfect fascination whenever someone played the piano. "Let me try. Let me try," I would say.

Mrs. Seymour, our family friend and nanny, adopted me as her pet and often took me home on Sundays, where I would anticipate playing her piano until dinnertime. I remember she told me repeatedly that someday I was going to be a great piano player.

My kindergarten teacher would let me sit at the piano with her and play the opening march when our class would file in for the day. I do not remember, but I suppose I played with one finger and a great big smile.

Someone donated an old upright piano to our family, and we started lessons from Mr. Tony, an eighty-year-old teacher who had the patience to teach and give piano recitals. I soon abandoned the music books and started playing everything "by ear." It was easier and much more satisfying. One of the first pieces I could play with both hands was "Under the Double Eagle." It sounded so big, bold, and brassy.

Like most small boys, I loved trains, planes, and automobiles. However, airplanes really got my attention. I must have been five years of age when I knew I liked airplanes. What a thrilling sight to see a plane up close. Someday I would fly in one, and maybe even be the pilot. Our community was only thirty miles from Ft. Benning Army Base. I remember large squadrons of military aircraft flying over our house. How exciting to see the sky filled with the sight and drone of their engines as they flew over. I would run back inside to play "Under the Double Eagle" as loud as I could.

Music was something I could do. It gave me my earliest identity. My social life blossomed with the piano. It was my first hobby. Having two brothers and four sisters, I treasured my time alone when I could explore the possibilities and wonder of the keyboard.

Little did I know that the piano and the airplane would be so dominant in my life, pushing me in two different directions and vocations. They would require different dedication and understanding; they would bring joy, challenge,

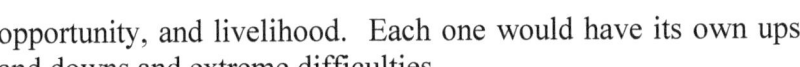

opportunity, and livelihood. Each one would have its own ups and downs and extreme difficulties.

It is significant that the week after my graduate orals and piano recital, I took my first flying lesson. It was my reward to successfully completing my graduate studies.

My first flight instructor, Fred, was skeptical and hard-nosed. His method of instructing was to tell you what to do without showing you. Then he would yell and say, "No! Do it this way." I successfully cranked the engine of the little Cessna 150, taxied out, and took off with minimum help from him. He told me that most of his first-lesson students did not return for their second lesson. He said, "I'm here to see if you really want to learn to fly—and to keep you from killing me."

After we were airborne, he took the controls and performed stalls, spins, and recoveries, showing me how I could actually kill myself. Finally, I told him I was feeling queasy and needed to land. But he had not deterred me from flying. I was determined to get my license, even if it meant learning to fly with a bucket between my knees.

Before I could schedule my second lesson, Fred died tragically in an early morning crop dusting accident. There was shock around the airport. He was known as an excellent "stick." It gave me pause to think how such a thing could happen to an experienced pilot.

My desire to learn to fly was the primary step toward licenses and flight ratings in my bi-vocational career, which would eventually result in my impossible dream of a career with a major airline. Meanwhile, I would enjoy a parallel vocation in education and church music for twenty years, while dreaming about airlines.

Just securing a pilot interview with a major airline was a seeming miracle. With fourteen thousand applications on file, how do you make yourself visible? How do you present yourself that sets you apart from the big stack? What do you bring to the table? How do you even get to the table?

I had seven thousand flight hours and all of the required flight ratings, people-management skills, college degrees, aviation system knowledge, a flight engineer rating, was able to pass background checks, and had a clean civil record. I was physically fit but had no heavy airplane experience.

The competition is fierce, and if you are lucky enough to get hired, you still have initial training and a full year of probation to navigate. At forty years of age, I was an unlikely candidate to ever be hired by a major airline. I had turned down lesser job offers and received multiple rejection notices all through my thirties. But I ached for the dream job.

Had it not been for the sense of calling and satisfaction of my bi-vocation of church music and aviation instructing, my fleeting dream could have debilitated me. I saw the window of opportunity closing, but issues of age discrimination kept the door slightly open. The airlines were hiring again. It was with my wife's encouragement that I made up my mind to cross every *t* and dot every *i* and go for it. If I qualified myself and it never happened, I could be happy.

Could I secure an airline job at my age? Could I ever have a life at 35,000 feet?

INTRODUCTION

WE TOOK OFF FROM CHICAGO O'Hare in the sunshine, headed for Miami. As we climbed through fifteen thousand feet, we knew we were headed for two long lines of active weather, a strong cold front with embedded thunderstorms, and a leading-edge squall line on the other side, all moving southeast. The storms had tops to 45,000 feet and severe weather all along the huge front.

Although we could not yet see the lines of weather, we knew that tornados had popped up from Kansas to Ohio during the early morning hours. This would be a day to keep your eyes on the skies.

I stretched forward to turn on the radar and hit the test button to run through the returns and Doppler functions. After a few seconds, the "radar fail" indication light came on. I turned the unit off and started the process over. It failed a second time with a "radar in opt" message. Our radar was dead.

I said to my crew, "Well, we may need to return to O'Hare. What do you guys think?"

The first officer replied, "I don't feel good about flying into that line without a radar unit that we can trust."

"That weather front extends all the way out past Oklahoma City," the second officer said.

"Well even if we could visually pick our way through it, we have to penetrate that same weather on the return trip this afternoon," I added. "Let's go back and get it fixed."

We all agreed.

I looked out and saw the beautiful, sunny skies we were flying in and hated to explain to our passengers that we could not continue due to the severe line of weather ahead. However, we would return to O'Hare now and avoid diverting later to someplace we did not want to go. I would explain to them that it would save time and fuel and give them more options and choices. I felt confident that a radar change would get us on our way again within an hour or so. Besides, we could not attempt to penetrate severe weather without our "sacred" radar.

It was a team decision to return to O'Hare, made in accordance with the flight manual. It is called "flight discipline." You see, we do not fly solo. Some decisions are already made for us.

Of course, we had skeptics on board who scoffed that bad weather could not be everywhere. To that objection I replied that we also could not be all over the map! We did have our flight plan route and limitations. The important thing about this flight was resolving our radar problem early, which would preclude solving new problems later.

This is true for our spiritual lives as well. We often taken hits from skeptics for our diversity from one church group to another. But the common ground we all share is the very basis of the truth we trust and believe. We have our "flight manual." We need not complicate our flight. Until we deal with our radar, we are fooling ourselves in sunny skies.

We live in uncertain days, but we do not fly solo. We fly in aviation community. That is our strength. We live our faith together. We are not all over the map. It is the "sacred" that we hold on to while we keep our eyes on the skies.

PART ONE

A DEFINITIVE BEGINNING

ONE OF MY FIRST MEMORIES is when my mother found me outside in our front yard as a two-year-old toddler, sitting on the grass with a light bulb in my hand. Unnoticed, I had escaped through an unlatched screen door to discover my first wonder. Shortly after, I was swept up into the arms of my mother, who wondered how I had gotten there.

That must have been the beginning of a realization. I was not totally in control of my wants and desires. I would learn that the authority in my young life was largely the loving, firm hand of my dad and mother.

My twin sister and I never lacked for attention as we grew older. With seven siblings in the house, we learned that our freedoms were granted as long as we followed the number-one rule: obedience. Moreover, it was expected from us. We learned that we could earn favor with each other by following the house rules.

However, simply keeping the rules did not bring happiness. It only kept us from fighting.

There was something beyond house rules. We were taught the importance of respecting authority, of knowing right from wrong, and how to keep the Golden Rule.

Another thing we knew for sure was the order and structure in our house. I knew we would have three meals each day and that I had a place at the table. Neighborhood play would end, and I was expected to be there. I also knew there would be clean-up chores before we left the kitchen and most probably, I would be involved in some manner before evening activities.

My mother had the patience that my dad lacked. He wanted action before he could show any patience. Perhaps he was reacting to scenes of his childhood. As I look back, I believe he feared everything could be a crisis unless he acted to prevent it. Once he saw obedience from his children, he relaxed and became loving, kind natured, and even jovial. But none of us doubted that he was the authority in the house.

THE AUTHORITY OF GOD'S WORD

"Then Jesus said to them, 'Walk while you have the light, lest darkness overtake you; he who walks in darkness does not know where he is going'" (John 12:35 NKJV).

THE GROUND CONTROLLERS AT CHICAGO O'Hare Airport are the best in the world. O'Hare is the busiest airport in the world. I was based there nine years and remember well many times how gridlock was avoided with timely and urgent radio commands on 121.75 megahertz.

One rainy night after pushing off the gate, with heavy radio chatter and waiting for clearance for twenty minutes, the terse voice in my earpiece said, "United 234, taxi runway 22 left, echo five, hotel, papa, outer bridge, join mike at tango ten behind a Delta heavy, hold short of Zulu, *Go now*!...break... In other words, "Do not read back the clearance."

I was a new first officer; I glanced at the captain. He pointed at me and nodded, so I replied, "United 234 roger, will co! (This meant we understood and would comply. We didn't expect that clearance, but now was not the time to figure it out with our airport chart.) "Go now; taxi now." That was the key phrase. In other words, "I know you have waited twenty minutes, and I have devised a plan for you, so don't mess it up." You could mess up another dozen airplanes. Moreover, we knew well, the tower was watching all of us.

Go now! It was a word of authority and immediate, imperative action.

The Bible, if it is anything, is a book of authority. It is not a book of suggestions, not a book of instructions, not "you might consider this," but it is the authoritative word of God.

Some Bible translations diminish the sound of its authority, but nonetheless, it's not the sound. God always speaks with authority. The Bible does not show the way, does not suggest a way, but declares emphatically that Jesus is the way. Jesus spoke the imperative word to Thomas when he said, "I am the Way, the Truth and the Life" (John 14:6 NKJV).

Follow me. Go now!

Go now! I heard those words often as a youngster. Go now, do this, do that. It was automatic to take that first step, even while stamping my foot and whining. Three stamps and three whines were generally one too many.

We all lived with a basic knowledge. Being one of seven siblings meant that if I got my way one out of seven times, I was doing fairly well. I do not remember when it became clear to us, but we were somehow aware that life was not a happening. It was a journey with challenges, surprises, failures, and triumphs. Moreover, we would begin to pull on our end of the rope and carry our part of the load.

BACK TO BASICS

Staying with the basics is not easy.

WE ARE OFTEN IN GREAT need of getting back to basics in our living. Each New Year reminds us about our priorities, diet, exercise, and goals. We resolve to do better, to get back to basics.

Genesis 1:26 tells us that God created man in his own image. Wow! That makes us basically unique with God. It is attributed that John Wesley said that man—even fallen man—is the only creature that is "capable of God." God brings us back to basics.

For example, airline pilots operate airplanes in what we know as "normal operations." If an emergency is declared, after landing, the airplane will be grounded. The entire scenario will be investigated and the airplane and flight crew debriefed before returning to normal basic operation standards. Only then can they fly again.

Our lives are complicated, and a return to basics is essential in avoiding breakdown or dysfunction. We will all experience catastrophic events in our lives, but we have hope when we render ourselves to God.

In Mark 12:17, the Pharisees were trying to trick Jesus with their question is it right to pay taxes to the Roman government or not, but he brought them back to basics when he said, "Give to Caesar what is Caesar's and to God what is God's."

Our lives are always in need of basics, which we cannot ignore without peril. We are designed for basic, normal operations. Abnormal ideas and beliefs will always get us off base—off basics.

There are many religious, non-scriptural practices and just plain weird ideas being cast about in our religious worldview today. They invade our lives and churches. Someone is always running an enticing idea up our flagpoles to see if we will salute it. Staying with the basics is not easy.

The Apostle Paul sternly reminds all, not just believers, "For since the creation of the world his invisible attributes, his eternal power and divine nature have been clearly seen, being understood through what has been made, so that they are without excuse" (Romans 1:20 NIV).

We are created in God's image and capable of God. We have God's Word. We are without excuse. We need daily reform…back to basics.

CLIMBING LIKE A HOMESICK ANGEL

"And God said, let the water teem with living creatures, and let birds fly above the earth across the expanse of the sky" (Genesis 1:20 NIV).

"The heavens proclaim the glory of God. The skies display his craftsmanship" (Psalm 19:1 NIV).

THE BAD PART OF BEING an airline pilot is that you can be the first to arrive at the scene of an accident. But the great thing is that you are the first to arrive in brilliant sunlight when climbing out of a low, dark, overcast sky after a foggy takeoff.

Could I take give you a ride on the flight deck? Come on in! Here we go… One final pull on the seat belt, cabin secure, checklist complete.

We are cleared for takeoff on a foggy morning. We push the throttles up and start down the runway. You hear the first officer say, "Eighty knots…thrust set, instruments cross-checked." As we gain speed, he says, "V one…rotate."

With that, the captain firmly moves the yoke aft and the nosewheel breaks ground. "V two…positive rate, gear up!"

And we are on our way up. The ground machine is now a space machine. You can't see out, and you feel your head swimming.

It can be foggy for thousands of feet. We raise the flaps, set climb power, contact departure control, move a few switches, complete the after-takeoff checklist, and accelerate to 250 knots. At ten thousand feet we can accelerate to max forward speed. That's when it gets fun, climbing like a homesick angel in the soup.

As we climb, suddenly it starts getting light, and without warning, we break into brilliant, blinding, exhilarating sunlight, clear of all clouds. The turbulence suddenly goes away, the flight is smooth, and we are outrunning the roar of the jet engines.

We've already put on our sun visors and sunglasses, expecting God's glorious beauty to appear. What a thrill! The cloud deck is quickly receding below. It is powerful and beautiful beyond description. It is a "longing," a yearning fulfilled!

As my pilot friend Dwight, said, "How can anyone resist the God of all light and creation like this?" And my soul sings the gospel song:

> Heavenly sunlight, heavenly sunlight,
> Flooding my soul with glory divine.
> Hallelujah, I am rejoicing!
> Singing His praises! Jesus is mine!"
> (Lyrics by Henry J. Zelley; published 1899)

> "Oh Lord our God, how majestic
> is your name in all the earth!
> Oh Lord, we magnify your name,
> Prince of Peace, almighty God!"
> (Lyrics by Keith Green)

LONGING

I can only try to relate to you how music and aviation became a part of me. It was a longing. *Sehnsucht* is the prominent German word. It means longing, desire, yearning, wishfulness, and aspiration. I believe everyone has a longing in their soul for the seeming unattainable. It is a human trait. We feel it in our innermost being as sweetness and a pursuit. We are windborne along by its taste. It is a wonderful gift from God.

From my early youth I dreamed I was a pilot. As I entered my teen and adult years, this *sehnsucht* became a driven force that seemed unreachable. However, I was gifted with music, a natural longing, you might say. Why should I desire to embrace aviation? Was it only a childhood fantasy like trains, planes, and automobiles?

It is for sure as years pass, the mysteries of our lives unfold. We come to know them as important events. As we tell the stories, the narrative of our lives becomes clearer.

Music and aviation were driving forces in my life. It is my purpose to relate a part of this narrative with interjected stories.

My dad impressed on me in my youth that I was exceptional. We all think we are exceptional. We want to be exceptional. "The rules do not apply to me in my particular case," we say. We can handle that circumstance. Why should we worry about the rules that govern everyone else?

Merely keeping somebody else's rules is no way to live, I thought. *Some way, I can figure this out for myself. If I am exceptional, I need to fly by the seat of my own pants.* However, in order to do that, you have to have money.

What did I really want out of life? The answer came back strong—happiness! What made me happy? Music did! If I could do music, surely the money would come. Did it really come down to music or money, happiness or wealth? One thing was sure: get your education first. Maybe I would find the flight plan for my life.

"Getting wisdom is the most important thing you can do! And whatever else you do, get good judgment" (Proverbs 4:7 NLT). "For I know the plans I have for you," says the Lord. "They are plans for good and not for disaster, to give you a future and a hope" Jeremiah 28:19 (NLT).

THE GOONEY BIRD EXPERIENCE

WHEN I STARTED COLLEGE, all male students were required to sign up for a year of ROTC (Reserve Officers' Training Corp). From the ranks of ROTC, you might have an opportunity of fulfilling your military obligations as an officer.

During our first year of ROTC (pronounced rot-cy), our squadron commander offered some of us a flight in the right pilot seat of the C-47. Although it had been two decades, this Douglas aircraft had been the main transport plane of World War II. I thought it was one of the most beautiful airplanes ever designed. Fifteen of us accepted the recruitment offer.

The C-47 airplane is affectionately called the "gooney bird," Our squadron commander promised that we would experience weightlessness for up to twenty seconds on this flight. The colonel would dive the plane to build up airspeed, then climb rapidly, nosing the aircraft "over the top" while we recruits would float free in the cabin, simulating weightlessness.

Manned space travel was in full development, and it sounded exciting.

We would have to wear our uniforms, and those of us under the age of twenty-one would supply a permission note and attend the recruitment and briefing session before the flight.

I was excited! I had flown three or four times with my friend in his Cessna 172, and I thought I could fly practically anything now. I was toying with the idea of joining the air force, but I knew that an interruption of piano study before graduate school would seriously jeopardize completing my master's degree in piano performance.

It was a hot and humid summer day when I drove out to Van de Graff Field for the "gooney bird" flight. The cumulous clouds would supply plenty of air pockets and bumps to make the ride even more special.

We all reported to the briefing room and practiced our weightlessness formation and positions. Then we marched to the airplane and received briefing on the sidewall bucket seats and seatbelts. It was 110 degrees in the cabin, and I was anxious to get airborne for cooler air. The engines suddenly roared to life, and before I realized it, we were airborne.

Our first maneuver attempt at weightlessness was aborted because of a large cumulous cloud that prevented its completion. My budding airman comrade in the front of the line suddenly strapped himself in and proceeded to throw up his lunch in his lap. The stench in the cabin was immediate. By this time, we were in the second dive and pull up. As the aircraft nosed over, the fourteen of us standing slowly went weightless and floated in the seated position, awaiting gravity's pull. Our flight commander counted a full seventeen seconds before we found ourselves back on our feet and scurrying back to our bucket seats.

By this time, some of my ROTC buddies were turning pale in the hot stench of the cabin. The instructor passed around buckets. Some of the fellows were unable to take their turn at the wheel as they delivered their lunch into the buckets one by one. I quickly volunteered to take my turn on the flight deck to get out of the putrid air. Only five of us got to fly that day, and

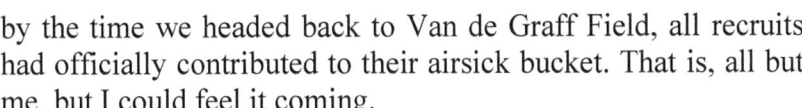

by the time we headed back to Van de Graff Field, all recruits had officially contributed to their airsick bucket. That is, all but me, but I could feel it coming.

We were on final approach. Still, I held on. Other recruits were egging me on as the final holdout. We landed and taxied to the ramp. The instructor opened the door and lowered the stairs. Everyone headed out the door, in need of fresh air. I finally stood and was the last to deplane. As I reached down for the handrail, I felt the hot, fresh air in my face. With all my comrades watching—and without warning—I did my first heave. Then with all my comrades cheering, the second wave hit me and I heaved it all over the steps and concrete.

I had not disappointed them.

However, it at was at that moment that I declined ROTC and decided to go for my master's degree in piano after graduation. My love for the piano sonatas of Beethoven had temporarily trumped my plans for flying.

"Trust in the Lord with all your heart, and lean not on your own understanding. In all your ways, acknowledge him, and he will make your paths straight" Proverbs 3:5-6 (NIV).

MERELY KEEPING RULES

THE TERM "SCRUPLES" IS AN old English term which is rarely used anymore in our society. It means the "fair and moral rules of human behavior." Our grandparents would say things like, "He has no scruples," or, "Where are your scruples?"

Of the hundreds of essays and articles written by C.S. Lewis, the shortest is entitled "Scruples." This essay goes straight to the gentle and red-hot words of Christ when he spoke and forever welded the Ten Commandments to the New Covenant: "By this all will know that you are my disciples, if you have love for one another" (John 13:35 NKJV).

Here is the short but burning essay of Lewis in its entirety, as addressed to us and about the Pharisees, the keepers of the law, in the New Testament.

SCRUPLES

> One mustn't make the Christian life into a punctilious system of law, like the Jewish, (for) two reasons.
> One, it raises scruples when we don't keep the routine. Two, it raises presumption when we do. Nothing gives one a more spuriously good conscience than keeping rules, even if there has been a total absence of all real charity and faith.
>
> C.S. Lewis (1898-1963, Letters to an American Lady, Wm. B. Eerdmans Publishing, 1986, p.38)

The commandment to love our neighbor as ourselves overrules and makes redundant the matrix of laws devised by a careless society.

The following story illustrates the two points raised by Lewis.

A young pastor once preached to his congregation that he believed God was telling him that for the next ten weeks every member of his church should commit to being in church every time the door was open. There are two wrong assumptions this pastor could have made.

> Those parishioners that did not keep that routine spirituality and concern for the church might be questioned.
> Those that did keep the routine could be presumed to be righteous before God, even in lack of real charity and faith and personal disobedience to him.
> In both cases, he could be wrong. It is clear that we are to keep God's rules.

FLYING BY THE SEAT OF YOUR PANTS

WE HAVE ALL HEARD THE expression "flying by the seat of your pants." This expression came from an earlier period before electronic navigation, full instrumentation, or systems operation was necessary. Modern technology requires a thorough understanding of the rules.

*Following rules can either
obscure or enhance the law.*

There are Rules, and there are Laws. The Rules made by men believe they are the experts and know best how to fly your airplane. They invent systems that you must master. The Laws of flying are made by God. You can—and sometimes should—suspend the rules of flying, but you cannot suspend the laws of flying.

It is important to know how to fly by the seat of your pants. Otherwise, you could find yourself in a nosedive.

Following rules can either obscure or enhance the law. The same is true with religious systems. However, following rules can never make us spiritually right with God. We must delight in his law by day and by night: "Blessed is the man that sits not in the seat of the scornful…but his delight is in the law of the Lord, and in His law he meditates day and night" (Psalm 1:1 NKJV).

God has put eternity in the hearts of man. His law is supremely higher than all the rules of man: "He has made everything appropriate in its time. He has also set eternity in their heart, yet so that man will not find out the work which God has done from the beginning even to the end" (Ecclesiastes 3:11 NASB).

DISCERNMENT

Moving through the shadows is better than stopping in the darkness. "He also brought me out into a broad place; He delivered me because He delighted in me" (2 Samuel 22:20 NKJV).

HAVE YOU EVER FELT CLAUSTROPHOBIC? Oh, the joy of being brought out into a broad place!

Several years ago, during one of those long air traffic control delays, we were in a long line for takeoff at Chicago O'Hare Airport. A lady on my airplane became short of breath and panicky, demanding to be taken off the airplane because she had become claustrophobic.

As captain, I asked the flight attendant to bring her up to the flight deck and I would explain to her that we could not taxi anywhere…we were stuck in traffic, now number four for takeoff.

This, of course, was before 9/11, and I asked my first officer to open his side window and allow this passenger to sit in his seat and stick her head out into the fresh breeze until we could move the airplane. Her panic attack started subsiding, and she assured me she needed to continue to New York.

Tight places, high walls, stale air, and the metal tube of an airliner make a poor personal perspective. This passenger had discerned fear and danger and had lost a sense of reality.

What is discernment? Webster's Dictionary defines discernment as: "1, to perceive by sight or some other sense; 2, to recognize as distinct or different; 3, to apprehend."

> *Discernment knows what happened*
> *without needing to know why.*

Driving east out of the Rocky Mountains toward Denver some sixty miles away on I-70 gives one a sensation that the mountains will never end. Although you are constantly losing elevation, there are mountain peaks and narrow valleys and twists constantly in front of you. You drive forty miles in these mountain passes, and then suddenly you arrive at a distinct change of terrain where twenty miles ahead and two thousand feet below you see the Denver terra firma floor. You suddenly apprehend or discern the enormity of what has been behind you and the beauty of what is before you. It is a change of perspective.

I would add another definition to Webster as it relates to spiritual discernment: To know without understanding why. You experience more than just a change of personal perspective; you have a sense of discreet knowing.

Winston Churchill is credited with saying, "Men often stumble over truth and then pick themselves up and hurry off without knowing what happened."

Discernment knows what happened without needing to know why.

God does not waste his treasures of wisdom upon the proud, naughty, or sinful. His wisdom is hidden. First Corinthians 3:1 reminds us that people who aren't Christians

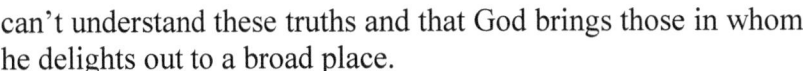

can't understand these truths and that God brings those in whom he delights out to a broad place.

We must not be static or paralyzed by fear. Moving through the shadows is better than stopping in the darkness.

> Prayer: Lord, give us the faith to move on. For those who love truth, discernment is just ahead.

THE FLIGHT PLAN

All of life is a ceremony.

There is a "flight plan" for our lives: "For I know the plans I have for you, declares the LORD, plans to prosper you and not to harm you, plans to give you hope and a future" (Jeremiah 29:11 NIV).

HIDDEN SOMEWHERE DEEP AT EVERY airport terminal is a place where all movements of aircraft from gate to destination are planned. This place is flight operations. It's a place of certain ceremony repeated thousands of times each day. After all, pilots are ceremonial people. There is a "sacred document" produced there called the Flight Plan.

The ceremony of the flight plan cannot be overstated. This is literally true. The flight crew arrives at the briefing room, and the flight papers are delivered to them. This is a legal packet governed by worldwide civil law (ICAO). It contains all information available everywhere as to the planning of that one flight. The joviality and mirth of the crew is temporarily suspended as they pore over these exhaustive papers.

This includes terminal and enroute weather, turbulence, planned altitude, aircraft history, and deferred items, route of flight, checkpoints, fuel requirements, and fuel burn.

Finally, after making desired changes, the captain, with ceremony and divine-like movements, holds up his pen, looks at his flight crew, and with an almost imperceptible nod of agreement signs the flight plan. This triplicate document is then separated and the first officer ceremoniously delivers a copy to the flight operations desk. The wisdom of the captain has now determined how that aircraft will sustain flight as it moves from

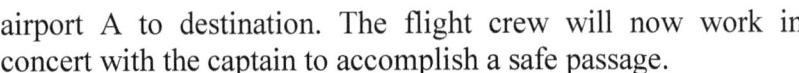

airport A to destination. The flight crew will now work in concert with the captain to accomplish a safe passage.

All of life is a ceremony. The wisdom of God has foreordained that we celebrate life from origin to destination. In it we will find meaning in joy or sorrow, through smooth or turbulent times, avoiding the storms and dangers that would destroy us and getting to know and love the Captain of our soul.

FLIGHT CANCELED

"But those who wait on the Lord shall renew their strength; They shall mount up with wings like eagles. They shall run and not be weary. They shall walk and not faint" (Isaiah 40:31 NKJV).

WE ARE CHRISTIANS IN THE MAKING. Maybe that is our divine appointment.

God, you say "wait." So who is in control? Those who wait or those who do not? Sometimes it seems that God's plans for our lives are not working out. What happened to all that ceremony I felt as I signed our flight plan? Now all my planning and attention to detail were coming to naught! I could hear the announcement: "Flight canceled. See the gate agent for alternative travel plans."

That night we were scheduled for a flight from Chicago O' Hare to New York LaGuardia. After dutifully planning a hard instrument flight plan into miserable weather conditions all along our route, including the eastern seaboard (not an unusual condition), we backed off the B11 gate to start our three engines one hour behind schedule.

Then we found that the number-one generator would not come on line. We accomplished the abnormal generator reset checklist. It was no help. With 150 New York passengers aboard trying to get home for the night, I knew immediately that we faced a hard decision that most likely would cancel the flight.

Although the airplane was still legal for dispatch, conventional wisdom of night flying into poor-weather destination airports with a severely limited electrical system was not something this young captain aspired to. Just minutes before, I had greeted the passengers on the intercom and thanked them for waiting patiently for this aircraft to arrive. I had assured them that we would make every effort to get them to New York City as quickly and as safely as possible. However, now we had an inoperative generator.

I quickly assessed that it would probably require a three-hour generator change if it could be accomplished at all that night. After talking with maintenance, I was informed that it was not possible but that the airplane was still legal for dispatch, and indeed, the company needed the aircraft for the first flight back the next morning.

As I looked at that yellow caution light indicating an inoperative generator, I felt the pressure of becoming a heroic captain and, against my better judgment, to continue on to New York. However, in that kind of weather I could imagine a stray static discharge knocking out another generator.

We do not always see the total picture, but that night I decided not to try anything legal or heroic. Safety and heroism do not mix well in an airplane. My judgment that night would be made on the ground, not in the air. So I canceled the flight and we walked out. I saw the pain and displeasure of the 150 passengers as they deplaned that night with no available travel plans. Later that night, as my flight crew left in the van on the way to the layover hotel, we encountered a horrific electrical storm as we left O'Hare. Someone spoke up and said what we all were thinking: "I'd rather be down here wishing we were up there than be up there wishing we were down here."

It was a tough decision, one I really did not want to make. We pilots train to handle those situations. I felt a bit like a coward. However, I walked off the airplane with the disciplined mindset of a captain in the making.

We are Christians in the making. Maybe that is our divine appointment.

Scripture says, "Wait upon the Lord to renew your strength" Isaiah 40:31 (JKV). I think this also means putting aside your strength and relying on the Lord while you wait. Kicking and squirming in the gate while you wait is not waiting at all…maybe "walking" is waiting.

Go ahead; make that decision…and you will find peace. Wait, and put God in control. Wait…and take his strength. Walk, and do not faint.

LET US LAY ASIDE EVERY WEIGHT

"Therefore, seeing we also are compassed about by so great a cloud of witnesses, let us lay aside every weight, and the sin which doth so easily beset us, and let us run with patience the race that is set before us" (Hebrews 12:1 NCV).

I WAS IN THE FLIGHT planning room at the San Jose Airport that sunny afternoon. We planned to takeoff at maximum allowable gross weight, headed toward the deep freeze and ice-covered airports of the mid-continent. Our destination was Denver, and I was not satisfied with our planned fuel. I calculated we needed an additional five thousand pounds for contingency.

Every airport from Salt Lake City to Omaha was snow packed, foggy, and they were getting worse. I explained to our disinterested dispatcher that our legal alternate Omaha was four hundred miles from Denver, but our contingency fuel was not adequate.

Our faith does not need to be analyzed so much but to be practiced boldly.

Our dispatcher complained that with every seat taken he would have to remove forty passengers to accommodate the extra fuel. I looked at the load manifest and suggested that we stay in the people business. Instead, maybe we could remove five thousand pounds of mail in order to add the extra fuel I had requested.

"But, Captain," he said, "we make more money on that mail than all of the passengers." "Let's just send the mail on the next flight," I patiently suggested.

He hesitated. I could sense he did not believe the extra fuel was necessary and did not want to take the delay. At that point, I patiently urged that we might as well get started on it. I would accept the delay and we would not go until we had the fuel. I was not popular, but I did prevail.

Since then, Hebrews 12 has loomed large in my spiritual thinking. Let me paraphrase it for this story: Seeing that we were compassed about with a great cloud of passengers, we laid aside the weight that beset us and patiently flew the delayed flight set before us.

I would like to tell you that we landed in Denver that night. We did not! But I will say that extra fuel was the best ground decision I ever made in my airline career. Well, whatever…that's another story.

This is for sure: We the Church need to stay in the people business. We gather with a great cloud of witnesses in our midst. We need to lay aside every weight that would hinder us and put aside the sin that so easily besets us…gets us off track. We need to run patiently the race that is set before us.

Our faith does not need to be analyzed so much but to be practiced boldly. The tormented soul that cannot make a decision is sorely crippled.

INDECISION

"Then the servant with the one bag of silver came and said, 'Master, I knew you were a harsh man, harvesting crops you didn't plant and gathering crops you didn't cultivate. I was afraid I would lose your money, so I hid it in the earth. Look, here is your money back" (Matthew 25:24-25 NLT).

WHY ARE WE SO INDECISIVE? Is it because we do not trust God?

I have a lot of sympathy for this servant. He was afraid, perhaps paralyzed with fear. Not knowing what to do, he played it safe. He was indecisive. Surely he knew his indecision would be accounted for when his master returned. But who knew when the master would return?
There is no place in airline operations that pilots can enjoy the luxury of indecision.
Once the airplane is in flight, a pilot's talent cannot be hidden in the ground in fear. Prompt and correct in-flight decisions have to be made. There are inherent dangers in the nature of flying.

"What if the master returns early?"

There are some decisions in my life that I will never forget! Here is the rest of the story from the San Jose flight.

That night, after airborne delays, we were descending in icing conditions over the mountains, approaching a foggy, icy Denver airport. We were at eleven thousand feet. It was 10:00 p.m. and the master did return early. We experienced a flap problem, with no time for indecision or becoming paralyzed with fear.

Now, pilots will understand high fuel burn at eleven thousand feet in icing conditions while accomplishing an abnormal asymmetrical flap checklist. It leaves no room for indecision or delay. Contingency fuel disappears like a vapor. We had no time to waste!

Landing in Denver with poor runway braking action and no flaps was now out of the question, even though dispatch wanted the airplane in Denver. I had insisted on five thousand extra pounds of fuel, the best ground decision I ever made.

We checked the weather quickly from Omaha to Albuquerque to find the nearest suitable airport. Nothing suited me, but there was a small weather opening in Colorado Springs. We decided to go for it.

My first and second officers had ten talents, not just one, and their talents paid off that night.

We accomplished the abnormal flap checklist and prepared for an asymmetrical flap landing. My second officer briefed the flight attendants and passengers and monitored our systems. The first officer relayed our plans to the company and dispatch and monitored the radar while I flew and planned the approach with air traffic control. We were busy, but we were unified, and now, we were the best of friends.

With the gear down and checklists complete, I saw the faint lights of runway 35L in Colorado Springs one mile ahead, and we landed into a forty-knot snow-blowing blizzard, wind straight down the runway. The landing was uneventful, just what we wanted, and just what our decision was all about. Colorado Springs was like home that night!

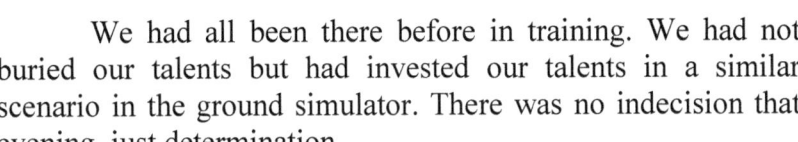

We had all been there before in training. We had not buried our talents but had invested our talents in a similar scenario in the ground simulator. There was no indecision that evening, just determination.

Later, at 11:00 p.m., I took the flight crew (all eight of us) to dinner and charged it to the company. We laughed, reviewed, and debriefed. We prayed, "God is good, let us thank him....and he's not a hard man!"

Why are we indecisive? Is it because we do not trust God? Brennan Manning, in his book *The Ragamuffin Gospel*, says:

> "Our indecision creates more problems than it solves. Indecision means we stop growing for an indeterminate length of time; we get stuck. With the paralysis of analysis, the human spirit begins to shrivel... Most of us postpone a decision hoping that Jesus will get weary of waiting and the inner voice of Truth will get laryngitis."
> The Ragamuffin Gospel; Multnomah Publishers (2000)

So why do we not trust God? We trust those whom we love. Yes, we do. God wants us to love him so we will trust him.

Prayer: Lord, without your help, we cannot love you as we should. Help us. Give us love for you so that we will trust you in every decision. Amen.

> "Fear not. Lo! I am with you, always"
> (Matthew 28:20 NKJV).

ARE YOU A FUNDAMENTALIST?

"And do not be conformed to this world, but be transformed by the renewing of your mind, that you may prove what is that good and acceptable and perfect will of God" (Romans 12:2 NJKV).

DO NOT LET THE WORLD squeeze you into its mold. We Christians have allowed the secular world to redefine fundamental Christians as somewhat backward, bigoted, and rigid people. This unfortunate redefining has been helped along by postmodern, free religionists that reject authority of Scripture and attack basic Christian practice.

A pilot friend once asked me if I was a fundamental Christian, and I said, "Yes! But I dare say that you do not understand what a real fundamental Christian is."

It was once an honorable term that spoke of basic tenets of Christianity, the authority of Scripture, and Christ-likeness that we should live out in our relationships with others. Christians hold themselves accountable to a personal style of living. Not perfect, but fundamental and full of grace.

I told my pilot friend that he was a fundamentalist also. I pointed out that he knew that Boeing Aircraft Company had built certain undeniable design into the aircraft systems we were flying; that these systems work according to their design and must be operated within the parameters of their design. If you don't follow these parameters, these systems will fail to operate.

I said to him, "You must be a fundamentally trained pilot, operate with fundamental knowledge, in accordance with the fundamental design. You understand and abide by these fundamentals, don't you?" For example:

- We pilots cannot exceed a maximum 8.6 psi (per square inch) differential on the cabin pressure controller. This means we cannot fly higher than 42,000 feet, or even lower if certain panels are placarded.

- We have a limitation on our taxi and takeoff weight.

- We cannot takeoff in surface temperatures above 118 degrees Fahrenheit, like on a hot summer afternoon in Phoenix, without over temping our engines.

- We abide by these fundamentals, and if complex systems fail, our basic fundamentals are even more important.

Pilots know that danger is real, the operating handbook is our authority, and its instructions can be trusted for a safe outcome of our flight. We trust our handbook.

Christians know that sin is real, Scripture is our authority, its instructions can be trusted, and our outcome is safe in heaven. Christians trust the Word of God.

Pilots and Christians both think objectively and with clarity because we believe in fundamentals.

Christian fundamentals are not ideas that have been muddled or confused by the media or humanists in the last twenty years. But it is living within the original teachings and parameters of God, the Master Designer, who came to redeem fallen man and give us safe flight from this world.

"Don't copy the behavior and customs of this world, but let God transform you into a new person by changing the way you think" (Romans 12:2 NLT).

Do not let the world squeeze you into its mold.

NO COCK AND BULL

AIRLINE PILOTS, BY NATURE, ARE hard to deceive or amuse. They can be a steely bunch. I have flown with hundreds of flight crewmembers. I have never been forward or obtrusive with my faith, but I have never tried to conceal it either.

Flying with the same flight crewmembers, the door is sometimes opened for religious discussion. Here is one such story.

Over dinner one evening on a layover, Jim began, "Renda, you seem to be a believer. What are you, Baptist?"

I answered, "It really doesn't matter, but you are right, I am a Christian."

He continued. "My wife is a strong Southern Baptist Sunday school teacher. She drags me off to church with her occasionally. It amuses me. They are always trying to convert me, but I don't believe that cock and bull Bible stuff," he said in a steely sort of way.

I smiled back and said, "Well, I suppose I don't understand the Bible as well as you because I do believe that cock and bull Bible stuff. Tell me, as you studied it, what did you find the central message of the Bible to say to you?"

He paused and looked at me. He did not know what to say. It was priceless! He finally answered, "It's about all that stuff you have to do to get to heaven."

I responded, "No, that's the cock and bull stuff! Let me tell you the good news, the news from the Book of Life."

1. The Bible is God's prophecy to his people that happened with the promised coming of his Son, Jesus the Messiah.

2. It was prophesied that Jesus would die on a cross for our sins and rise the third day to give us eternal life.
3. He ascended back to the Father in heaven and sent his Holy Spirit to assure us of his lordship in our lives.
4. In that eternal day he will return for us and judge the world of sin and righteousness. We only must repent and believe.

"Miraculous? Yes! The resurrection of life? You bet! Christianity is the only religion that makes these claims.

"That's what Baptists believe, and that's what I believe...belief in the divine Son of God, the Creator of the universe, who also redeems us to get us to heaven.

"Now, Jim, I know there can be a lot of cock and bull that goes on in churches...like our golf game yesterday. But the Bible is documented history, revealed in the ancient books of Hebrew, the study of the Roman Empire, and the canons. It is a miraculous story you have to believe by faith. I suggest you read your Bible in faith. It is not a story to deceive or amuse you."

Jim was thoughtful and appreciated my words.

Here are some wonderful scriptures that sum up the essential message I tried to give Jim that evening. Read them with joy!

Romans 1:1-4; 1 Corinthians 15:2-4; 1 Timothy 3:16; Philippians 2:5-11

STRAPPING ON THE YOKE

"Come to me, all you who are weary and burdened, and I will give you rest. Take my yoke upon you and learn from me, for I am gentle and humble in heart, and you will find rest for your souls. For my yoke is easy, and my burden is light" (Matthew 11:28-30 NKJV).

THE FIRST THING AN AIRLINE does when he sits down in the cockpit is get himself yoked to the airplane—he adjusts his seat, fastens his seatbelt, and adjusts the rudder pedals for easy full throw in case it becomes necessary. Then he pushes his seat back and forth and up and down for security and comfort. He is getting comfortable so he can feel in unison with the yoke.

We call it "strapping on the airplane." In other words, we fly and the airplane and people are strapped to us. The pilot simply cannot fly until he secures this position. In the basic sense of the word, this is airmen-ship 101.

The airplane is providing all the power and lift. We are in unison with the airplane, holding only a light touch on the

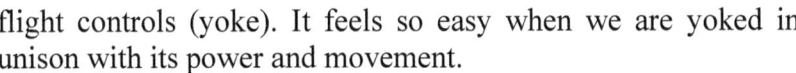

flight controls (yoke). It feels so easy when we are yoked in unison with its power and movement.

I have often had people say to me, "I don't see how that big thing can fly." Or maybe this: "The takeoff is the scariest part for me. I strain and just can't let my weight down for the first few minutes."

I smile. We really want our passengers to sit back and relax and enjoy the flight.

Matthew 11:28-30 describes this desire for our customers. When Christ tells us to take his yoke and learn from him, he assures us that his yoke is easy and his burden is light. He provides all the power and lift. There is no reason for us to strain or try to do the lifting. We just need to get in unison and agreement with his yoke…and feel his power.

THE GREATEST MOMENTS

*Oh, the newness of flight into
the heavens with God!*

There are two moments that a pilot lives for.

First, the moment when on takeoff, after power is set and the aircraft is approaching V-one speed, it becomes apparent that the airplane will soon become a sky machine. The callout procedure goes like this: 80 knots, instruments cross-checked, thrust set...then faster, faster...V- one...go-no go decision...V r...rotate. At this instant the pilot removes his hand from the throttles and with both hands smartly muscles the control yoke back several inches toward his stomach. The massive longitudinal fuselage begins a rotation toward twelve degrees, nose up. The nosewheel breaks ground and enough lift is generated within seconds to lift the four hundred-ton airplane into the air.

What a rush, sitting atop a powerful aluminum tube of fuel and flesh!

The pilot suddenly feels like a god. Friction with the earth is lost, and the acceleration is exhilarating...positive climb. The captain calls for gear up...flaps five...green light...flaps two...green light...flaps up, set climb thrust. What romance! The captain is invincible! I liken this to the defining moment in the life of the Christ follower when the new Christian life loses friction with earthly things, his soul rushes to heavenly realms, and he suddenly feels the very heart of God himself. His new soul seems invincible. Oh, the newness of flight into the heavens with God! What acceleration! What romance! "Not by works of righteousness which we have done, but according to his mercy he saved us..." (Titus 3:5-6 KJV).

However, there is an even greater moment of flight—a much more somber and sanctified moment—when landing conditions are below the personal allowable demonstration of the pilot. This is the moment that with trepidation the captain must engage the autopilot for an auto-coupled approach down to minimums below his instrument limits.

With feather-light touch on the controls, the pilot must feel the muscle of the flight guidance system as it manipulates inputs to the flight controls. How humbling it is to trust the auto-coupled system as this unseen hand edges the aircraft down into the darkness of the unseen runway. But how wonderful it is to trust the guidance system he relinquishes in his hand! All fear is cast out, and the holy "moment of truth" occurs when the environment of the runway comes into view.

What a sanctified moment it is when the Christian also comes to know this relinquishment, submission to the perfect love of God. "Sanctify them through Thy truth: Thy word is truth" (John 17:17 KJV).

PERSEVERANCE

THE STRING OF TOWNS THAT comprised the Chattahoochee Valley where I grew up were located along old US Highway 29, a route made famous by President Roosevelt when he would travel to his summer home near Warms Springs, Georgia. The townspeople of West Point, Lanett, Shawmut, Langdale, and Riverview would line the highway to cheer President Roosevelt when his entourage would travel to or from the "Little White House."

Although the towns were small, its people were very proud. My friend Comer Jr. lived in Shawmut. I lived two miles away in Langdale. Comer recently reminded me that Shawmut people never begged Langdale people for anything. We were taught to let other people recognize you, not to call attention to yourself.

It affected the way I applied for a flying position with the airlines. Airline pilots do not land in great jobs unless they sell themselves to a prospective employer. A holy dedication of earning thousands of hours of flight experience and flight ratings precedes a major airline job. You must persevere and be lucky as well. You do have to get attention. You have to promote yourself to get your application on top as more qualified without bragging or begging. I had never learned how to do that because we were too proud to sell ourselves.

As a young teen, I quickly learned that life would pass you by if you did not compete. Find your gifts, your talents, and go for it. My gift was music, but I had another love…airplanes. My head was in the clouds!

Although I found success and fulfillment in directing a large church music ministry, only my wife, Sharon, knew of my deep, unsatisfied longing to have an airline career. At times, I

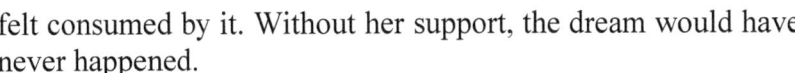

felt consumed by it. Without her support, the dream would have never happened.

Then, at the ripe age of forty-four, my childhood dream came true. So do not give up on your dreams!

Persevere! Trust your dreams! Be bold! Never stop dreaming. You can change your life. "Let us run with endurance the race that is set before us" (Hebrews 12: 1 NKJV).

PILOT FATIGUE

*Lindbergh had started out with
no other goal but to arrive.*

CHARLES LINDBERGH MADE HIS HISTORIC solo flight from New York to Paris in May, 1927. His 3,610 mile nonstop crossing of the Atlantic took thirty-four hours and most of the 451 gallons of fuel he carried.

Can you imagine a dark, foggy night with the drone of a loud engine over endless ocean followed by sleepy eyes looking into a bright, rising sun, dead reckoning to an unfamiliar landing strip, still over one thousand miles ahead? Yet, there was another night to come and a night landing to execute.

Lindbergh expected to experience fatigue. He wrote the following in his flight log:

> My mind clicks on and off... But the effort's too much. Sleep is winning. My whole body argues dully that nothing, nothing life can attain is quite so desirable as sleep. My mind is losing resolution and control.

But Lindberg had started out with no other goal but to arrive.

Today, federal regulations require airline pilots and air traffic controllers to be rested before accepting an assignment, but regulations are not enough. Law alone is never enough. Pilots must exercise good judgment if their rest period is inadequate. Passengers expect their flight crew to be rested and up to the job.

Many of us are running on unending materialistic treadmills that just go round and round, faster and faster.

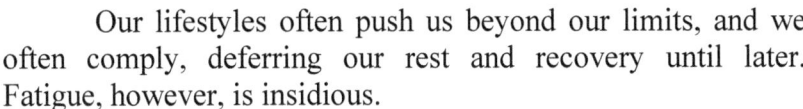

Our lifestyles often push us beyond our limits, and we often comply, deferring our rest and recovery until later. Fatigue, however, is insidious.

How often do we say harsh words when we are fatigued? We operate our business affairs, interact with people, and make important decisions when fatigue might affect our judgments or relationships.

How often would it help to say to each other, "Let me help you," "You are too fatigued," or, "Have you thought of this?" Also, we need to learn to say, "Sorry, I have too much on my plate at this time."

We need to step off the treadmill.

Scripture says, "Come unto me and I will give you rest."

We start the Christian life with but one goal: to arrive.

"My presence will go *with you,* and I will give you rest" (Exodus 33:14 NKJV).

"Return to your rest, O my soul, for the Lord has dealt bountifully with you" (Psalm 116:7 NKJV).

These verses tell us that we do not fly solo. When fatigue would overtake us, we can rest in the Lord.

EMPTY TANKS

Our lives may look great to our friends, but we cannot operate spiritually on empty tanks.

YEARS AGO, I FLEW A corporate flight of executives to Scottsdale, Arizona. Due to the passenger load, I planned the flight for legal minimum fuel. Upon landing, we discovered that refueling was not available until the next day (but that's another story!). We were grounded for the night. I thought to myself, *That's a great, shiny-looking jet airplane out there on the ramp, but it is useless without fuel.*

I peered into the fuel tanks and confirmed that there was limited combustion for those engines. The plane was out of service. The fuel on the airport was contaminated and not trustworthy.

That afternoon after a short drive, I visited "the Bone Yard" at nearby Davis-Montham Air Force Base, where thousands of military aircraft of all sizes and descriptions are parked and retired in obsolescence. Their fuel tanks are empty. Vents, panels, and doors are taped shut to keep sand and dust out of systems in order to preserve their airworthiness should the planes ever need to be inspected and filled with fuel and flown again. Those planes look great, but what a useless fleet of technology—empty tanks, empty airplanes.

The maintenance of our spiritual lives is much the same way—sometimes empty and out of service, unable to carry payload.

Our lives may look great to our friends, but we cannot operate spiritually on empty tanks. The blind cannot lead the blind unless they both fall into the ditch.

The Word of God ignited by prayer is necessary for spiritual combustion to propel us into action and service as we allow God's Spirit to fill us.

Ephesians 5:18 says be filled with the Spirit, God's command!

AIR TRAFFIC CONTROL COMMUNICATION

AIRLINE PILOTS ARE THOROUGHLY SCHOOLED in flying and aviation knowledge, but without learning the practical art of air traffic control communication (ATC), all of their training is useless.

I remember my first flight into Chicago O'Hare airspace. I was a rookie corporate co-pilot, a slow-talking southern boy, a lost soul flying among professional airline angels. I quickly had to learn to listen intently and to talk twice as fast as I ever had before, praying to get it right the first time.

Radio communication is much like a language of prayer, a practice of listening and speaking, understanding and complying with ATC while enroute to destination. Every moment of flight requires constant radio monitoring (communing) with this unseen authority.

King David said, "In my distress I called upon the Lord and cried out to my God; from his temple he heard my voice, and my cry reached his ears" (2 Samuel 22:4 NAB).

We are not aliens with God.

For the Christian, prayer is the practice of monitoring, communing, listening, and speaking to God. Prayer is the authority that God uses to guide us in our journey.

My first trip into Chicago O'Hare, I felt like an alien in hostile airspace. I did not have a prayer, and I felt like crying, "Help!" In fact, I admitted to ATC that I was not familiar with O'Hare procedures.

Approach control reassured me, "Radar contact. Don't you worry. I'll get you there."

The controller reconciled me into his traffic flow. He said, "Keep your speed at 210 knots and follow that 'United traffic' at your ten o'clock position. He's going to your runway."

I thought to myself, *With a prayer and his guidance, I can make it.*

Jesus reminds us that we will not be heard for our words, but for whom we are speaking to.

ATC is the authority for the pilot. Likewise, God is "the Whom" for the Christian. "Be anxious for nothing, but in everything by prayer and supplication, with thanksgiving, let your requests be made known to God; and the peace of God, which surpasses all understanding, will guard your hearts and minds through Christ Jesus" (Philippians 4:6-7 NIV).

We are to pray without ceasing, and indeed, our best prayers are when we cry for help and guidance.

We are not aliens with God. We can never escape his Love. He is the "hound of heaven" and is always seeking us. His mercy is everlasting! It is unending, relentless, unceasing, forever. No arbitration needed!

FALSE RADIO COMMUNICATIONS

"Dear friends, do not believe every spirit, but test the spirits to see whether they are from God, because many false prophets have gone out in the world" (1 John 4:1 TNIV).

ONE OF THE IMPORTANT ISSUES of Air Traffic Control (ATC) is guarding against false radio commands from illegal transmitters and unknown voices. These voices can cause havoc and great danger when a pilot is led astray by following wrong instructions. My ATC friend Dave told me an airline pilot reported strange voices and rap music on his radio over Oklahoma City.

Shortly after the horrific events of 9/11 on a flight to Dulles, ATC issued us a magnetic heading that I knew we could not fly very long. It took us straight toward prohibited airspace in Washington, DC, so I questioned ATC if this was indeed the heading they wanted. I certainly did not want an F15 fighter pilot to come alongside ready to take action against us. It was my responsibility to confirm the voice of ATC, recognize their phraseology, and know my flight position in relation to the published route.

There have been documented instances where airliners have received false instructions by ATC imitators trying to divert them to a mythical course.

The ultimate source of false doctrine is Satan himself.

Jesus said, "My sheep hear my voice and I know them, and they follow me" (John 10:27 NKJV). The sheep hear and know the voice of the Good Shepherd. Likewise, it is spiritually

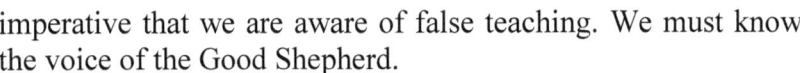

imperative that we are aware of false teaching. We must know the voice of the Good Shepherd.

Truth mixed with error is sometimes more dangerous than error itself. The New Testament warns the churches about false teaching: "These teachers are hypocrites and liars. They pretend to be religious but their consciences are dead" (Timothy 4:2 NLT).

The ultimate source of false doctrine is Satan himself, promoted by those with spiritually dead consciences. They often claim that their teaching is super-Christian when it is sub-Christian at best and far from true gospel.

Today, with the diversity of every man's truth, we must know and follow sound doctrines. "For the time will come when people will not tolerate sound doctrine but, following their own desires and insatiable curiosity, will accumulate teachers and will stop listening to the truth and will be diverted to myths" (2 Timothy 4:3-4 NAB).

The antichrist described in Daniel 7, 8, and 9 could soon appear.

MIDDLE C

We need a "middle C" in our lives.

My mother loved to read when she could afford the time, but with seven children in the house, reading was the second priority for her. I clearly remember when she read *The Robe*, an immensely popular book in the religious community when I was a child. She wanted all her children to read this book when they were older because it was the core values of our faith. Written by Lloyd C. Douglas, a minister of the gospel, it told the story of the crucifixion and resurrection of Jesus. It is a universal story. It is our story. The book gained even more popularity when the movie version was released in 1953.

I recently read *The Robe*, and I also learned this interesting story on the Internet about the author.

When Lloyd Douglas attended college as a young man, he lived in a boarding house next to a retired music professor who was impaired in a wheelchair. Each morning he would check in on the old professor and ask him, "What's the good news?"

The professor would pick up his tuning fork, strike it on the arm of the wheelchair, and respond, "That's middle C. It was middle C yesterday; it will be middle C tomorrow; it will be middle C a thousand years from now. The tenor upstairs sings flat. The piano across the hall is out of tune. But this, my friend, is middle C."

The world in which we live is out of tune. We need a "middle C" in our lives. We need a standard by which to measure all other things and to bring stability in a swirling, deceitful, changing world that lies to us.

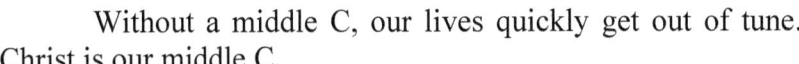

Without a middle C, our lives quickly get out of tune. Christ is our middle C.

We also need to be a middle C in the lives of others whom God entrusts to us.

I challenge you to strike the tuning fork often and keep your life in tune to God's song.

"Listen, my son, and be wise, and keep your heart on the right path" (Proverbs 23:19 NKJV).

CORE BELIEFS

CHRISTIAN CORE BELIEFS ARE NOT negotiable. If we try to negate or negotiate them, something will quickly go wrong.

When I was in high school, a substitute teacher taught our chemistry class one day. I am not sure how it happened (someone said the teacher did it), but a small clump of pure sodium was tossed into a beaker of water. The resultant explosion and fire at the front of the room sent us all scattering.

In life, there are not any spectator seats.

I went out the back door into the hall shouting, "Fire!" Other classmates more intelligently poked their heads into classrooms down the hall, telling students, "Fire! Get out!"

Someone broke the glass in the fire alarm, and the entire student body filed out, laughing as if it were a fire drill. The school principal shot out of his office, thinking, *Aha! Another false alarm prank*! When the fire engines showed up a few minutes later and smoke was pouring out the second-story classroom window, everyone became keenly aware that it was no fire drill or false alarm.

We all went home for the rest of the day with a new appreciation for practice fire drills and lessons learned.

> *Lesson One:* It does one no good to have core beliefs and not practice them in one's particular discipline, chemistry class included.
> *Lesson Two:* One must know his core beliefs, particularly if he teaches chemistry.
> *Lesson Three:* One must not just accept core beliefs but also know their implications.

Lesson Four: Don't let a substitute teacher with limited knowledge decide your core beliefs.

We also learned that day that we all were on common ground, whether we were in the chemistry class where the fire started or in the adjacent building where the fire alarm also rang. We all soberly participated!

Eugene Petersen says, "There are not any spectator seats… Wisdom insists that nothing in the human experience can be omitted or slighted if we decide to take God seriously" (Introduction to the Wisdom Books; The Message).

> Today's culture tells us that core beliefs are intolerant and politically incorrect. But God's Word tells us, "Do not become so well-adjusted to your culture that you fit into it without even thinking. Instead, fix your attention on God" (Romans 12:2 MSG).

THE MAIN THING

SUCCESSFUL PEOPLE KNOW THAT IN every endeavor the main thing is the main thing.

Often in our attempt to achieve our objective, we let other ideas clutter the main objective. Not all ideas are equal; the main thing is the main thing.

Such was the case years ago when I flew my brother's Cessna 172 to Charleston, South Carolina. I knew I would need fuel before returning home, so I planned to stop short of my destination at an unimproved airport (grass field) where fuel would be cheaper. I would use my pilot skills and execute a short, soft field-type of approach and landing.

My first mistake was to assume that all unimproved airports are equal. They are not!

In retrospect, grass runways are charted as unimproved airports. That's a concept in itself. "Unimproved" is another word for "unknown." I intellectually knew the difference, and looking down from a distance, the grass runway looked fine. But my touchdown and landing on the rough dirt path was more like a controlled crash. After two surprise bounces, I got serious, saved the landing with a burst of controlled power, and fortunately, nothing got bent (except a wheel cover).

However, I would face that rough surface again on takeoff.

When I walked into the small frame building that served as a fuel station, I saw a wall of pictures showing airplane mishaps in the area. Some rested in trees, some flipped over, and others had bent wings. I could see my wife and two-year-old toddler back at home in the background of every picture. I thought about turning in my flying license and trucking the airplane out.

I discarded all the other ideas I had (buying cheaper fuel, playing around with unimproved airstrips, etc.) and went for the main thing: getting out of there alive.

I decided not to buy the fuel, not to add the weight. That could wait until later.

After walking the entire 2,500-foot airstrip into the wind, I found the smoothest path to the left of the main landing area that I would use for takeoff.

The final step was to determine my density altitude takeoff distance to a height of fifty feet to clear the tall trees at the end of the airstrip. I opened the flight manual to the takeoff performance section. Using the current temperature, soft-field takeoff technique, and max power (leaning the fuel mixture), I determined it could be done. I then selected a visual point at which I would need to rotate to get airborne or otherwise abort the takeoff. I did all of this with my new friend, the proprietor pilot, looking dispassionately over my shoulder. His last words to me were, "Yes, I could personally do it myself, but it's up to you, buster." I looked over and saw his camera lying on the counter.

The main thing became the main thing. Forgetting the main thing is always a compromise. Do not intellectualize yourself into a compromise. Stay with the main thing.

To save fuel cost, I had stopped short and settled for second best.

Sometimes the same thing can be said about our spiritual lives. From a distance, we look fine, but when we get down to it, the unimproved dirt paths we travel show the great need for improved surfaces. In a sense, the Holy Spirit, our helper, is available, but he is inaccessible in our compromise.

Perhaps we all need a time in our spiritual lives when we decide we will not compromise for second best.

We suffer from a new age, non-biblical thought that says that we should not take ourselves so seriously. We hear it in sermons and read it in popular Christian writing. But I don't find this idea anywhere in the Bible. However, I do find it easy to forget the main thing.

By the way, I cleared the trees at the end of the strip with a good margin of about fifty feet. Life is good.

DISQUALIFIED

I WAS A FRESHMAN AT the University of Alabama, and I had my binoculars trained on number 12, the great All-American from Alabama, Willie Joe Namath. He sidestepped a tackler and headed up field only to fall to the ground, almost untouched, grabbing his knee.

I said aloud, "He's hurt! He hurt his knee!" People sitting around me did not believe it, but Joe was out for the season.

Later, Namath was disqualified from military service with a 4F classification. He was, however, resurrected to a brilliant career in the NFL. Imagine that!

Being disqualified from flying is one of the greatest fears of an airline pilot. It can happen a number of ways: a careless act, lack of progressing in training or upgrade, incurring a flying incident or infraction, or failing to pass a first-class medical examination every six months.

I was once disqualified from flying for almost three months when I sustained a severe lower back injury. For weeks I could not sit or walk without pain, much less carry my flight bag.

When my neurologist released me for examination by the FAA medical examiner, it was with great apprehension and relief to watch him sign the return to flight status green slip. He smiled and said to me, "Get back on the flight line, boy!"

I had been resurrected to new life and was no longer disqualified. I felt the weak, unused muscles in my lower back spontaneously strengthen. I was going back to the flight line!

Standing before Jesus Christ, we are not qualified, not worthy to be called by his name. We do not upgrade spiritually. Nonetheless, Christ's resurrection gives us new life, new hope. "Therefore we were buried with him through baptism into death, that just as Christ was raised from the dead by the glory of the Father, even so we also should walk in newness of life" (Romans 6:4 NAS).

Christ's resurrection is our hope, our only hope. Through his infinite atonement and mercy, we are made worthy to be his follower, even his disciple. Not by our own efforts, but by his mercy he raises us to flight status in his kingdom. He puts us back on the flight line.

Whatever the reason we feel unqualified or disqualified, what joy it is to hear him say to us, "You have been resurrected to new life. Get up, my child, and get back on the flight line."

I urge you: fly the good flight and keep the faith.

WHAT DOES THE BOOK SAY?

How is the view out your windshield?
Is it foggy? What is your worldview?

We were at 33,000 feet headed to Newark when I suddenly noticed that the first officer's windshield had badly fogged over.

"Hmm, when did that happen?" I inquired.

"It was clear just a minute ago," the first officer replied. "Do you think we should descend?"

"Well, this can be more than meets the eye. What does the book have to say? Let's go to the irregulars and review the checklist first. Meanwhile, we can slow back to 250 knots. Feel your windshield. Does it feel as warm as mine?"

"No, it's cold," he responded. Just as I had suspected, our windshield heat had failed.

"We'll check the circuit breakers. Why don't you fly the airplane, and I'll review the book with Alan" (our second officer).

"Cleveland Center, United 638 here, we need to slow back to 250 knots, over."

It is prudent to slow to 250 knots with a windshield problem. All pilots know that at low altitudes heated windshields are designed to withstand a one-pound bird strike at 250 knots…or, we jokingly add, a 250-pound bird at one knot!

One of the first things a pilot does during his preflight check is switch on the window heat. Cold-soaked windshields are brittle. Window heat provides measured amperage, preventing overheats. Power increases as needed to prevent thermal shock as we rapidly climb to cold altitudes.

The irregular checklist did not solve our windshield problem that day, and our airplane had to be grounded after landing. Our passengers would be rerouted, and we had to endure a double deadhead to a new assignment.

How is the view out your windshield? Is it foggy? What is your worldview?

Are the warmth of God's Word and the fellowship of Christian community keeping you from becoming brittle? Have your circuit breakers popped, or has your windshield cracked? Is God's power increasing in your life as needed?

If we stay at low altitudes, we risk getting a bird strike, but we cannot fly at high altitudes without window heat. The heat of God's Word is our protection. See what the Book says. You will find help through the irregulars and can return to normal flight.

THE BLACK BOX

THE BLACK BOX IS ACTUALLY not black at all but rather an iridescent orange flight data recorder and cockpit voice recorder in a rugged metal chassis. Designed to withstand severe crashes, it records time, date, flight events, turns, magnetic headings, movement of controls, G forces, and cockpit communication by the pilots.

All commercial passenger aircraft are required to have a black box. In the event of a crash or damage to an aircraft, the black box is sent to the National Transportation Safety Board (NTSB) in Washington, DC to be analyzed by experts.

The black box is the conscience of the plane. A telltale story of what went wrong and how it happened can be derived from its extracted information. A flight scenario will be pieced together with a time code, and the tragic event can be examined and re-enacted with radio and cockpit conversations. The black box records the flight inputs and results in the same way our conscience judges our actions.

God knows our hearts. He knows what is in our black boxes.

Nothing is hidden from his sight. He knows our comings and our goings. He knows the wrong turns we have made. He knows the anguish and the turbulence that we have faced.

God knows and he cares. Our hurts matter to him. He is merciful. And he says to each of us, just as he said to the woman caught in sin and accused by the Pharisees, "Neither do I condemn you. Go and sin no more" (John 8:11 NKJV).

PART TWO

FLIGHT SCHOOL WITH GOD

Unproved assumptions are dangerous in the cockpit.

PEOPLE HAVE OFTEN SAID TO me. "Wow, flying the airlines! What a fabulous and glamorous profession, all that fun and travel!" Not so fast!
    Let me tell you a story.
My initial flight training at United Airlines was exciting, but much more was involved. I thought I was a good pilot. I had seven thousand flight hours, but that does not matter. This is where most people "wash out."
    The process that leads to the first time a newly qualified pilot walks into the flight deck of a major airline testifies to the blood, sweat, and tears already paid before he gets to that first revenue flight. He has undergone a purifying fire. He is dead serious about his flying, and his training never ends. Surprise FAA checks can occur anytime, and you can be grounded for many reasons.
    It is not cheap. It is very costly. The professional pilot gives up a part of daily home life, his family life, and social life with friends. He does not live a life of indulgences; he keeps his body in first-class condition.
    He is sober and serious about his accountability, reliability, and authority to the joy of releasing the parking brake and pushing up the throttles with a plane full of passengers. Then he comes back with new fortitude and joy to fly the next trip.
    The company owns him for about one hundred hours a week. Yes, he has atoned for his chance to fly.
    Unproved assumptions are dangerous in the cockpit. The pilot can lose his license at the whim of the FAA if he even appears to mess up. "Glamorous," you say. It is more like atonement every day.

After my initial training when I reported for my IOE (initial operating experience), I checked into the chief pilot's office in Chicago Flight Operations. Without blinking, the chief pilot looked me in the eye and said, "Keep your head down and your nose clean. You are at the mercy of many people this first year. You cannot mess up. You will need a spotless record. You'll understand that better by and by."

I remember the "come to Jesus talk" I had with myself after that meeting. Is this really for me? How badly do I want this? Is this what I have dreamed of all my life? Talk about atonement! I remember in a weak moment, I almost gave the whole thing up. I was reminded of the Apostle Paul's exhortation: "I beseech you therefore, brethren, by the mercies of God, to present your bodies a living sacrifice, holy, acceptable to God, which is your reasonable service" (Romans 12:1 NKJV).

The misunderstanding of the atonement of Christ for the sins of man has often become the basis for "cheap grace." If Christ has already paid the penalty for our sins, why should we bother about further practice in holy living? It is because the "cockpit of life" requires more.

Initial Christian conversion is wonderful, but the entry into "flight school with God" will cost you plenty in producing fruits of his lordship in your life. Staying in that relationship requires obedience that you've never thought of before. "What shall we say then? Shall we continue in sin? God forbid" (Romans 6:1 NKJV).

Sin is serious. We are no longer slaves to sin, but we are slaves to righteousness.

"Oh, the depth of the riches of the wisdom and knowledge of God! How unsearchable his judgments, and his paths beyond tracing out" (Romans 11:33 NIV).

His love has no limit; His grace has no measure,
His power has no boundary known unto man.
For out of his infinite riches in Jesus,
He gives, and gives, and gives again.
                Words by Annie Flint, 1866-1932

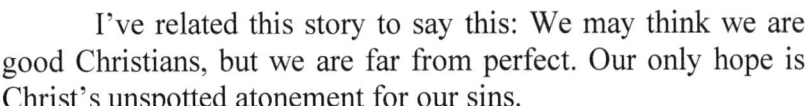

I've related this story to say this: We may think we are good Christians, but we are far from perfect. Our only hope is Christ's unspotted atonement for our sins.

BECOMING AN EXPERIENCED PILOT

"Blessed are the pure in heart for they shall see God" (Matthew 5:8 NIV).

Becoming is a word of action.

The joy of becoming a new hire with a major airline is an ecstasy that is impossible to convey except to another pilot. I felt as though I had been selected for astronaut training or something close. My year of hire included 250 of us selected from 14,000 applicants. It was a very becoming path to follow. Even though the first year is probationary, the smile on your face is difficult to wipe off. You are just happy to be on the property.

The hardest part of getting hired was passing the scrutiny of the human resources department. They considered people-management skills as necessary captain material. They were hiring more than just aviators.

While I held myself to high perfection in musicianship, I felt good about my easygoing people-management skills. I did not realize how exacting and demanding I would become in cockpit leadership management (CLM). It was necessary because there is a critical balance in achieving the most from your flight crew as you go around defying gravity for twenty thousand flight hours!

This is Kayla, age 5. She is becoming!

    I only relate this to make clear the reality that all new hires, while being considered "captain material," are apprentice pilots, and only after several years and thousands of flight hours will they have a chance to become a captain.

    The new hire has a sober consciousness of inexperience. They know that they must learn their company's FAA certificate of operation. Even then the process has just begun. It is not easy to become or remain a captain. And a captain does not smile easily with hundreds of lives in his hands.

> *The Christian life is not easy,*
> *not all smiles, and there is no*
> *stopping, only becoming.*

    When we are new-hire Christians (that is, born again), there is an ecstasy of the presence of Christ in our lives. We are just happy to be on the property. We are joyful apprentices. We have only just begun the process. We soon have a consciousness in our walk with Christ, and we know just how much our sinfulness has permeated our humanness.

The church has not always been clear about the work of the Holy Spirit in sanctification and purification of our minds and hearts and lives.

It is one thing to be forgiven of our sins but quite another to have our inner being sanctified and cleansed for the advanced and difficult path of following Christ. There is no cookie-cutter model to follow; we cannot do it within ourselves, and it is not always easy to smile when we are in the process of becoming.

When Christ said, "Blessed are the pure in heart, for they shall see God," he was not only giving us a promise but also admonishing us in our journey to submit to the work of the Holy Spirit, only by which we can become.

When I was a kid, there was a television show called *Queen for a Day*. There was no becoming process. You were suddenly picked and showered with gifts. And then it was over suddenly, just a fairytale. There was no becoming!

However, this scripture speaks of becoming: "And you, who once were alienated and enemies in your mind by wicked works, yet now He has reconciled in the body of His flesh through death, to present you holy, and blameless, and above reproach in His sight" (Colossians 1:21-22 NKJV).

The Christian life is not easy, not all smiles, and there is no stopping, only becoming. There is a daily walk, a holy path to follow, and a destination. It is submitting to Christ. It is the way of righteousness through Christ, the perfect sacrifice. Righteousness is becoming.

Become a captain. Be presented holy and blameless and above reproach in his sight.

"Faithful is He who calls you, who also will do it" (1 Thessalonians 5:24 NKJV).

THE AUTOPILOT

AFTER MY INITIAL LINE TRAINING, I quickly noticed that experienced line pilots exercised judicious and limited use of the autopilot when not at cruise altitude. It was hands-on flying that kept the pilot's flying skills sharp.

It is so easy to engage our spiritual autopilot and drift into euphoria with no one in command. It is a certain way to lose our spiritual awareness.

In 1999, professional golfer Payne Stewart and his pilots became euphoric and died from lack of oxygen during a rapid flight transition to high altitude. The autopilot had been engaged, and a pressurization problem was not caught in time. Tragically, extenuating circumstances contributed to the unpressurized cabin and subsequent crash. Hands-on attention is needed most during rapid flight transitions.

While the autopilot is an aid in precise flying and planning, today's autopilot systems arrest even greater control of flying skills. For the same reason, we need to keep our spiritual skills dedicated to hands-on flying.

Autopilot systems have been the culprit of notorious and catastrophic crashes. They can reduce situational awareness, and that is improper use. The proper use of the autopilot is to enable more vigilance and preciseness when needed. But dependence on the autopilot can reduce the hands-on flying skills of the pilot.

*Have you ever felt yourself
on spiritual autopilot?*

Have you ever felt yourself on spiritual autopilot? It can be a good feeling, but one must ask these questions: Am I drifting along, or am I aware and planning for the next spiritual transition that faces me?

We live in times of rapid transition. Sometimes we put our spiritual lives on autopilot and find ourselves off course and at risk with imprecise spiritual decisions.

How do you perceive your spiritual life? Is it on autopilot?

Challenge yourself. Don't become euphoric. Click off the autopilot.

FOR THE LOVE OF FLYING

"For the joy of the Lord shall be my strength" (Nehemiah 8:10 NKJV).

It is great to have future plans to look forward to, but it's even better to be content with today, looking forward to the present.

I WAS A NEW HIRE second officer on reserve in Chicago. My beeper went off, and I hurried to my crash pad to return the call, knowing it was the crew desk with a short-notice flying assignment. A three-hour callout was the norm, but they asked if I could get to the airport within the hour.

I said, "Yes, I can make it."

"Be there when the plane arrives to meet your flight captain and crew. That way the flight can still go out on time."

I donned my new uniform, grabbed my hat and flight bag, and headed out.

I will never forget the words the captain said to me as I met and joined the crew in the cockpit.

He glared at me and said, "You're a new hire, aren't you?"

I smiled and said, "Yes, sir! I'm glad to be on the property."

"I can tell by that smile on your face. Go do your aircraft walk around and try to leave that smile outside," he said as he looked away.

Puzzled, I glanced at the first officer. He managed a slight smile, shook his head with a knowing frown, and thumbed me toward the door. I set my flight bag down, grabbed my flashlight, and headed out for the exterior inspection, wondering, *What is going on here? No wonder the captain needs a second officer. The other one probably called in sick enroute and went home.*

Ninety-nine percent of all pilots love to fly, love their job, and cannot keep from smiling on the flight deck. However, I was in for my first rude awakening with this one percent sour captain.

About the only words the captain and I spoke were the perfunctory checklist responses and very little small talk. It was a long, three-day trip, but meanwhile, the first officer and I became good friends. I was happy to be flying and on the clock rather than alone or sleeping at the crash pad or wishing to be home with my family.

This captain definitely had some issues with joy and love for flying. He said he was counting down the days when he could retire. I wondered what he was looking forward to. He was sure missing a lot of living right now.

We can still find joy in life's uncertainties. We can experience love in the midst of sorrow. We all know someone whose hill to climb is greater than our own hill. Hope springs eternal in the heart.

It is great to have future plans to look forward to, but it's even better to be content with today, looking forward to the present. Somehow, you will find yourself counting your many blessings.

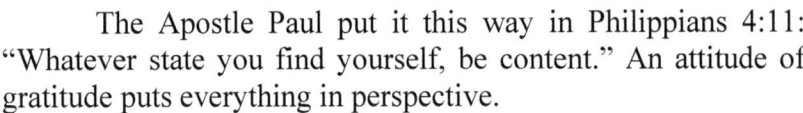

The Apostle Paul put it this way in Philippians 4:11: "Whatever state you find yourself, be content." An attitude of gratitude puts everything in perspective.

Whatever your hill to climb, you are not alone. The joy of the Lord shall be your strength. You can defy gravity. You can fly, even when it is tough.

AWAY FROM HOME AND COMMUTING

Faith meets the crisis of the moment.
Faith happens on the road.

AN ESTIMATE 40 PERCENT OF airline pilots in the United States are based in a domicile city in which they do not live. I can testify that a commuting pilot is an incomplete person, living a half-life, depending on memories of another life.

Many times I have run for an open jet bridge door after four days of flying, trying to catch the last plane home for my days off. Sometimes as I arrive at the gate I find the door shut. I am a commuter and have the authority for the jump seat, but I just missed the plane home. What a feeling of despair!

You suddenly feel like an unappreciated stranger in a strange land, knowing that the airplane is in sight but you missed it. Your authority is suddenly all gone. All the good work that you did in providing safe passage to hundreds of passengers that week now means little. You are no longer on the clock; there are no provisions made for you. Your work is done. You are destined to find transportation to unknown lodging for the night, hundreds of miles from home, where you want to wake up. It feels like despair…hell…separation. There is truly no place like home, but you missed your plane.

C.S. Lewis wrote of Christian sojourners when he said we are but strangers in a foreign land. This world is not our home. We are incomplete, living a half-life, depending upon promises of another life.

However, faith meets the crisis of the moment. Faith happens on the road. Faith occurs at the impact of the moment. Faith gets us moving again. And faith turns to hope for the next day's early flight home. Commuting home is the happiest event of the week.

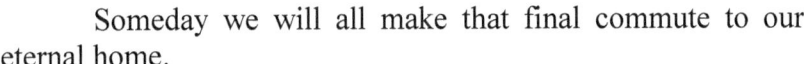

Someday we will all make that final commute to our eternal home.

My friend Comer, a boyhood chum, reminded me of this wonderful southern gospel song he sings around the house: "We'll have a grand homecoming week, the first ten thousand years." It is true.

Don't miss the plane.

> "Behold, I stand at the door and knock. If any man hears my voice, I will come in and dine with him, and he with me" (Revelation 3:20 NKJV).

Christ spoke of himself: I am the way. I am the door. I am the gate.

WEEDS

WE WERE TAXIING OUT FROM Manchester Airport heading for Chicago O'Hare when the control tower informed us that Chicago flow control had stopped all incoming flights due to bad weather. The control tower instructed us to taxi straight ahead and hold on the old ramp while awaiting further clearance.

As I surveyed the holding area, I remarked to the captain that I was skeptical of taxiing a 170,000-pound airplane on that old, suspect-looking ramp where grass and weeds were growing in the lines of concrete. He responded that it should be no problem since the tower had cleared us there. I was still skeptical, and I said so.

I was a new second officer. Why should the captain listen to me? Little did we know how prophetic my skepticism was that day.

We slowly entered the old ramp, and suddenly the airplane lurched hard to the left. The concrete under our left landing gear gave way. I dispatched out the aft air stair to survey what had happened. Luckily, pieces of extending steel rebar prevented the left landing gear from dropping into a six-foot deep hole; otherwise, it would have surely ripped the wheel assembly from the plane. Large gashes of rubber separated from the tires. This is the only time in twenty thousand hours of flight that any small part of my aircraft had ended up below the surface of the pavement. It was not a good feeling. That day, we had a brush with danger. We need to question our surroundings.

If you are taxiing on a good taxiway,
do not depart from it.

To this day, I do not understand why I was bold enough to question an experienced captain about taxiing our plane on that old ramp. It was not my wisdom. However, I do know that all wisdom comes from God. Jeremiah prayed, "I know, O Lord, that a man's life is not his own; it is not for man to direct his steps" (Jeremiah 10:23 NIV); "The steps of a good man are ordered by the Lord: and He delights in his way. Though he falls, he shall not be utterly cast down: for He upholds him with His hand" (Psalm 37:23-24 NKJV); "A highway shall be there and it shall be called the Holy Way" (Isaiah 35:8 NIV).

Do not taxi off into the weeds with your life even though someone in authority might say it's okay or even authorize it. Trust your conscience and your inner voice of reason. If you are taxiing on a good taxiway, do not depart from it.

Stay on the improved and trusted surfaces (the Holy Way). You do not have to accept every clearance or perceived freedom you feel. Question suspected ideas. Hold fast. Do not compromise. Listen to the voice of God. Consult, trust, and take advice from your real friends. You will avoid some trouble, and you may arrive at your destination sooner.

FINDING THE PEARL OF GREAT PRICE

> Jesus taught this parable: "Again, the kingdom of heaven is like a merchant looking for fine pearls. When he found one of great value, he went away and sold everything he had and bought it" (Matthew 13:45-46 NIV).

SO MUCH OF OUR TIME concerned with finding the right direction, the right school, the right job, the right mate, and the list goes on. That is the way it should be. The choices we make should not be based on a whim of the moment but with more thought for the future than what happens before nine o'clock tonight.

Often an airline captain will say to his passengers, "We will keep you advised." He does not make flight decisions by whim but by a process of choices that may take you beyond nine o'clock before destination is reached.

I remember many times as a first officer asking the captain, "What do you think? What heading should we take around those storms?"

Critical decisions are made in consultation with loved ones who can see what we cannot see. God's Word reminds us, "We set our eyes not on what we see but on what we cannot see. What we see will last only a short time, but what we cannot see will last forever" (2 Corinthians 4:18 NCV).

Our lives are full of decisions, so set your eyes on the ultimate goal. Commit yourself to it. Do not just seek the kingdom of God in your life. Seek ye first the kingdom of God. Sell all you have, and you too will find the pearl of great price.

THE FLIGHT DECK

I WAS A NEW SECOND officer en route to Chicago O'Hare when the ACARS (computer radio system) summoned me to a change in my flight itinerary. After arrival, I was to report to gate B16, where the plane, flight crew, and passengers were already loaded and ready to push off the gate. After landing, I quickly hurried to my new assignment.

As I headed down the B16 jet bridge, the gate agent implored me as to how long it would take to get the plane off the gate. I told her that it would take about twenty minutes. She seemed displeased with my answer and shocked that I would delay the flight for more than simply three or four minutes.

She knew little about the flight duties of a second officer.

- The required airplane walk around
- The flight-performance computations
- The system checks
- Arming myself with information to support the captain and first officer and getting into the loop myself.

At that point, I did not even know where this flight was headed. I rushed into the cockpit to drop my bags and join the flight crew. The captain greeted me warmly and introduced himself. "Glad to see you. Take your time on your walk around. We'll be ready to go only when you are ready to go," he instructed me.

God invites us to enter that far greater arena into his presence.

Upon returning to the flight deck after my walk around, there was a feeling, a presence in the cockpit that I liked. The captain again advised me, "Don't rush; get comfortable." I once again felt the serious business and joy of flying. This is what I had signed on for. The captain, with his understanding words and instructions, had quieted my spirit. Suddenly it did not feel so much like work.

I thought to myself, *This captain is someone I want to emulate—full of wisdom, understanding, and mercy.* I felt revived and anticipated our upcoming flights together. I knew I would enjoy this captain's flight deck.

On the other hand, what a clamoring culture we live in, making so many demands on our lives. We get so busy—school starting, new schedules of running back and forth, attempting too much. I sometimes think that if we ran the airlines as we run our lives, airplanes would crash and burn on a daily basis.

More than ever in these times we need the presence of God to quiet our spirit and renew in us the joy of living. God invites us to enter that far greater arena into his presence, to come with thanksgiving, trusting our lives to the Holy God who will order change in our flight itinerary.

God actually wants us to live in his temple; he wants us to be his temple. There is peace and order on God's flight deck. It is there that we can dwell in his holiness.

Prayer: Thank you, God, for your mercy and for your guiding hand. May we surely and quietly respond to your love. Make us holy and fit for your temple. Amen.

THE GLIDE SCOPE

*The guidance of the glide slope is
critical. Truth matters—all the time.*

IN AVIATION, A GLIDE SLOPE is an extended electronic beam that guides an aircraft along a precise path down to a safe landing point on the runway. Low-visibility landings can be accomplished in the "soup" if flown with preciseness from a known altitude.

A false high glide slope exists at a harmonic resonant of the true glide slope frequency. It can be subtle and deceiving.

Years ago as a new second officer, I encountered this false glide slope phenomenon, which until that point had been only theory to me. We were approaching Chicago O'Hare from the west, and the captain was at the controls of our 727. The overcast skies in which we were flying were reported at eight hundred feet above the ground. This instrument approach would apparently end with an easy visual landing.

As we were intercepting the apparent glide slope, we were cleared for the approach and advised to contact the tower. Approaching the outer marker, it quickly became apparent to me that we were about four hundred feet above our charted altitude. I immediately informed the captain that we were too high and posed the possibility that we had intercepted a false glide slope from our cleared position. I suggested that we execute a missed approach, to which the first officer agreed. At this point the captain seemed to be in denial of the truth, unaware of our position, and he arrogantly continued the approach.

A few minutes later, we broke out of the overcast conditions and the captain became a believer. We were obviously off the charted glide slope. We were too high, and a landing was not possible. The tower immediately issued a go-around procedure.

I had only known in theory the guidance of a false glide slope. Suddenly, without notice, it became a reality in the operational world. Knowing my true position was necessary. Communicating the truth to the captain was my job. The false glide slope was more than theory.

Were we about to crash? No. Were we precise? No. Were we deceived? Yes! Was I uncomfortable? Absolutely!

A friend recently told me of a situation in his life where he finally came to the reality of truth. I think he already knew the truth. He had been living on a false harmonic of the true glide slope for a while…not a good way to live!

We live in a vague, unbelieving, often arrogant world, but truth is not difficult to know. We have the clear, resonant Word of God. We cannot be in denial. We have our chart. We must know our position. The guidance of the glide slope is critical. Truth matters—all the time.

The glide slope is the way, the truth, and the life. No pilot comes to the runway but by me (John 14:6, my paraphrase).

HOLY DAYS

"Be ye holy, for I your Father in heaven am holy"
(Leviticus 11:45 KJV).

EACH MONTH, THE AIRLINE PILOT declares three "holy days" in his or her schedule of flying. The company cannot touch these days for reassignment, training, or travel. These holy days are set apart for family and known life events, for purposeful living, and planned events.

Purposeful holy living is God's standard of perfection for all of our days on earth. We are created in his image, just a little lower than the angels…just a little lower than God, according to the Hebrew. Anything less than his image is of our own making and separates us from God.

Since Adam, we are born with a sinful nature. God in his nature, which is holiness and love, through Christ transcends this gulf. We are rescued from our terrible predicament and can be rejoined in fellowship to God by the perfecting of our holiness: "For since by man came death, by man came also the resurrection of the dead. For as in Adam all die, even so in Christ shall all be made alive" (1 Corinthians 15:21-22 KJV).

We cannot declare ourselves holy. Only God can declare our holiness, our righteousness. But we can declare each day of our living schedule as a holy day, set apart. In Christ, our living is full, planned, purposeful, and alive. Moreover, Satan himself cannot reassign us. "Blessed are they who hunger and thirst after righteousness, for they shall be filled" (Matthew 5:6 KJV).

We need to declare our all of our days as holy days. That is the way to live!

> "Teach us to number our days, O Lord, and help us to realize how few they be. And help us to use them as we should" (Psalm 90:12 TLB).

THE TOUCHDOWN ZONE

I RECALL A HUMOROUS TOWER transmission as we waited number one for takeoff one morning. As we watched, a DC 10 landed long and hot and used the entire runway for stopping. The tower said, "Fedex, make a hard right turn at the end of the runway if able and contact ground twenty-one point nine. Good day." We chuckled at the humor. His alternate taxi instructions could have been, "Take exit 312 off the interstate and return to the airport."

Did you know that every runway approved for commercial air service has a touchdown zone (painted markings on the runway)? The paint starts at one thousand feet down the runway and includes no more than the first three thousand feet. Pilots must land in the touchdown zone or execute a go-around. Pilots know this maneuver as a "get out of there" procedure!

A go-around is a big deal to pilots. There are some inherent risks in executing a go-around, depending on wind, weather, terrain conditions, and proper execution.

However, landing before or beyond the touchdown zone has even graver dangers because you could hit obstacles short of the zone or land with unknown remaining runway and run off the end. Airline pilots must always work with known quantities. Otherwise, we become test pilots (temptation pilots) and that is not for airline pilots.

In Christian living, temptations are always an unknown quantity and a "get out of there" maneuver is needed. We should execute a go-around before getting to the unknown. It is not a sin to be tempted but only in yielding to temptation. If we will flee from temptation, God will provide a way of escape.

Part 61 of the Federal Air Regulations (FARS) state: During flight tests, the successful outcome of a flight maneuver must never be seriously in doubt. This means, the judging of a flight maneuver is concurrent even before the maneuver is completed. So if you are in doubt, the flight check airman expects you to discontinue the maneuver.

Christians can judge well in their hearts before the temptation is complete. Is there a worse place than the heart to be tempted if the outcome of that temptation is in doubt? God says clearly to us, "Discontinue. Flee."

I remember a landing on a 13,000-foot runway. The first officer was flying. It became obvious to him and me that he was going to miss the touchdown zone. He landed with a nice, smooth touchdown and slowed to a taxi speed and announced, "You've got the airplane, Captain."

As I took the controls, I quietly said, "You missed the touchdown zone."

He said, "Yeah, but I knew I still had eight thousand feet left."

He was an excellent pilot and a friend, so I said to him, "I don't think that's a proper response from a professional. What your flying comrades want to hear is, 'C'mon! Get it down, or we are going around.' He might add, 'That is not up to my standards, Captain!'"

Then he said to me, "You know, I saw the problem coming at five hundred feet in the air."

I replied, "Yes, and that is when you probably should have spoken up. Your next landing could be on a short 5,000-foot runway. Our standards must be high."

Likewise, Christians can see temptation coming from five hundred feet away. "Flee from temptation." Do not land. Go around. Get out of there!

When we got to the gate, the first flight attendant said, "That was a great landing."

The first officer said, "No! It was a terrible landing. It felt good, but it wasn't good."

We pilots do have help. In visual landing conditions, a complex arrangement of lights and mirrors (a VASI) guides us to the touchdown zone. In foggy flight conditions we have electronic guidance to the safe touchdown zone. But we must have the runway environment in sight, and our standards must be high. There can be no compromise!

We Christians also have help: "For we do not have a High Priest who cannot sympathize with our weaknesses, but was in all points tempted as we are, yet without sin" (Hebrews 4:15 NKJV).

If Christ is in our sight, we are in the touchdown zone.

WHO DO YOU TRUST?

Real truth protects us. Assumed truth is destructive.

THE TRAGIC CRASH OF AN attempted early morning takeoff of a regional jet on a wrong runway leaves staggering unanswered questions for highly trained airline pilots. It is so easy to Monday morning quarterback a tragedy like this because there were several assumptions made right before departure. Many pilots can say, "It could have been me but for the grace of God."

Here are some wrong assumptions made before the takeoff roll.

1. This runway is adequate in length and width.
2. This is the correct runway heading.
3. This runway has the proper paint and markings for a 7,000-foot runway.
4. Our magnetic heading is correct with the assigned runway.
5. My instrument departure setup is correct, indicating my departure path.
6. I see nothing wrong with this view out my windshield.

Assumed truth had crept into the cockpit. It was silently screaming, "No, false!" Situational awareness was lost, and attention to the very basics was compromised. These kinds of accidents don't happen suddenly but often have a progressive history.

This same incident almost happened in Lexington in 1993. In a letter filed in 1993 with the Aviation Safety Reporting System (ASRS), maintained by the National Aeronautics and Space Administration (NASA), another pilot described his experience:

> Aircraft was cleared for immediate takeoff (traffic was inside the marker) on runway 22 at Lexington. We taxied onto the runway and told tower we needed a moment to check our departure routing with our weather radar (storms were in the area, raining at the airport). We realized our heading was not correct for our assigned runway and at that moment, tower called us to cancel the takeoff clearance because we were lined up on runway 26 (the wrong runway).

What do we learn here? A wise instructor once told me, "Anytime you feel rushed to accomplish a task in the cockpit, stop. Verify. Start over and make sure you do it right. And hold your other crewmembers to the same standard."

That is pretty good advice for life also. I remember many times when we just slowed down a bit, looked around, reconsidered, and adjusted back to normal flow.

In this recent accident, there were a few signs along the way and no doubt some distractions. But the glaring mistake is the failure of the flight crew to hold each other accountable as they performed their final taxi and pre-takeoff checklist and while taking command of the flight.

Good friends sometimes do not hold each other accountable. Assumptions are allowed while incorrectly trusting each other. We must trust but always verify. Real truth protects us. Assumed truth is destructive. "The safest road to hell is the gradual one—the gentle slope, soft underfoot, without sudden turnings, without milestones, without signposts" (C. S. Lewis, *The Screwtape Letters*).

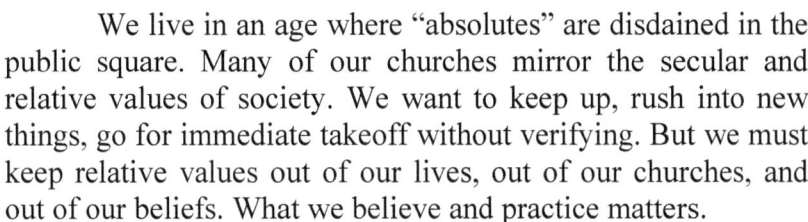

We live in an age where "absolutes" are disdained in the public square. Many of our churches mirror the secular and relative values of society. We want to keep up, rush into new things, go for immediate takeoff without verifying. But we must keep relative values out of our lives, out of our churches, and out of our beliefs. What we believe and practice matters.

Do not accept everything you hear from a television, from a pulpit, a platform, a Sunday school teacher, or a friend's testimony. Know what you believe. Scripture commands us to pray for wisdom. Avoid heresy, and "here say" beliefs. Stay with the basics. This is our day to get serious and not be deceived.

The Bible declares these truths: Broad is the way and narrow is the gate; there is a way that seems to be right to man, but therein is the way to destruction; there is one Way, one Truth, one Light; no man comes to the Father but by Me; not everyone who cries, "Lord, Lord!" will enter in.

Knowing what and who one trusts is not just good. It is imperative!

THE GLORIOUS GRACE OF
THE GOOD NEWS

I NEEDED TO FLY TO Denver for a quick trip. As I took my seat, I was thinking how wonderful to relax on God's terms for the next hour, knowing that I had avoided a twelve-hour drive.

As I was getting comfortable, a lady tentatively took her seat by me and said, "Flying scares me to death. I am praying for a miracle to arrive safely. I hate the takeoff and landing. I just can't let my weight down. How about you?"

I told her, "Well, I've flown more than twenty thousand hours as a pilot, and believe me it's much safer than getting on Interstate 40. Go ahead and relax. Let your weight down. You are avoiding a twelve-hour drive on God's terms."

It was apparent that our relationships with the same moment were totally different. She sensed danger and the unknown. She could trust only herself in fear. But I had total faith in the crew up front.

It's the same as we consider the gift of the good news of Jesus. The gospel of grace brings us up close with the mystery of intimacy of God in his forgiving love and care, rather than seeking for miracles and begging for salvation in fear and mistrust.

There is the often told story of a man who was overheard on an airplane during wild turbulence praying aloud, "God, get me off this airplane and I'll give you half of my wealth." A minister heard him, and after they landed he reminded him of his promise.

The man said, "I made God a better deal. If I ever get on another plane, I'll give him all of it."

Our solution is a Band-Aid. God's solution is a Spirit-filled life of grace, forgiveness, and healing.

Jesus brings us good news, not bad news. The good news is this: Jesus declares, "Your sins have been forgiven. Go and sin no more" (John 8:11 KJV). We do not have to strike a deal with God. He freely offers his saving grace, if we will believe in him. Your sins are forgiven. Now turn around, repent, and leave your sinning ways in belief on the love and mercy you have received. Go now. Faith has transformed you. Put your faith in action.

How difficult can we make Romans 8? Our solution is a Band-Aid. God's solution is a Spirit-filled life of grace, forgiveness, and healing. We are no longer on the terms of the Pharisees and the Sadducees, who depended on the law, or the terms of John, the son of thunder who wanted to reign down fire on the Samaritans. We are on God's terms.

Who can separate us from the love of God? The answer comes from the heart of God. He is the one who says, "Trust me only, love me only, and fear me only. I embrace you fully. Trust me!" Does that sound radical? It is radical. The grace of God is radical. It is everlasting and it is the power unto salvation. We must believe and live in his grace. It is the power unto salvation. Friends, believe the glorious grace of the good news of Jesus Christ. Your destination is ahead.

HAZMAT IN THE CHRISTIAN LIFE

THE TRANSPORT OF HAZARDOUS MATERIAL, abbreviated "hazmat," is now commonplace in the transportation industry. Hazmat is regulated through training and certified inspectors who verify shippers, proper packing, air handling, and notification procedures to flight crews. The danger is controlled in how it is packed, accommodated, and transported.

The captain can reject transporting any hazmat via his cargo bins when considering all other factors pertaining to his flight. As captain, I have rejected materials when I could not verify the shipper or type of material in question through flight manual information or our company inspector.

Unfortunately, we are faced with a wide array of hazardous materials and ideas in our Christian lives. It confronts us in daily living. It endangers our families, our values, and our commitments. Sometimes this hazmat can appear nonthreatening, commonplace, and innocent. How we control it is of utmost importance.

I relate this actual 1999 incident at LAX airport. While unloading a Northwest Airlines 747 from Japan, a cargo forklift operator damaged a large pallet of camera type, small, lithium-metal batteries, approximately 120,000 in number. Some three hours later, this pallet erupted into a 1,400-degree fire, which can melt any aluminum cargo bay.

This accommodation of hazmat appeared safe. It could have been disastrous. You can be sure this procedure concerning passenger planes has now been addressed. However, the clock may still be ticking on other issues.

Our lives and our families interface with vast unregulated hazmat in the vile attack on our damaged culture. We see it in the marketplace of entertainment: on television and in movies, in the music listened to, and in our schools. You can be sure the clock is ticking on this hazardous material in our culture. We must not carry this cargo in our lives but keep God's Word in our heart. "God is our refuge and strength. He is our help in times of trouble" (Psalm 46:1 KJV).

NEAR MISSES

*Like an optical illusion, it is
easy to miss the truth.*

Today we hear a lot about runway incursions and near misses in aviation. It makes for good media and newsprint. How many near misses have I had in aviation? I only know of four. Those occurred in general aviation, none in airline operations. Maybe there are more that I do not know about. Those are the scary ones. Nevertheless, every flight presents the possibility.

Do not ask a US senator or political operative to define or to correct near-miss problems. They will play politics, pass the blame, or create another pork-barrel solution.

Ask the air traffic controller, the person wearing the microphone headset with his fingerprints on the radar screen. They can fix the near-miss problem by 8:15 Monday morning. They know the truth. They know you must hire capable,

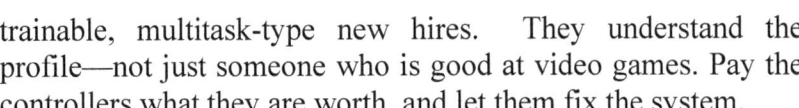

trainable, multitask-type new hires. They understand the profile—not just someone who is good at video games. Pay the controllers what they are worth, and let them fix the system.

With increased air traffic, we have the greater chance for midair collisions. Also with increased diversity of religious ideas and the postmodern idea of relative truth, we have greater chance for spiritual illusions and heresy.

How many misses have I had with the truth? More than I care to count. Those are the scary ones. How many times have I failed to acknowledge all the protections and many blessings of God?

A friend recently told me they have trouble believing in the nature of a vengeful God of wrath in the Old Testament. We should ask the men of the Old Testament as to the nature of God. Ask Moses, Joshua, Elijah, and Job. They know the truth. They put themselves into the hands of a merciful God rather than falling into the hands of their vengeful enemies.

King David said, "Let us fall into the hands of the LORD, for his mercy is great; but do not let me fall into the hands of men" (2 Samuel 24:14 KJV).

Like an optical illusion, it is easy to miss the truth. We tend to attribute to God our own human attributes. However, if we present ourselves to live under his sovereignty, we can know his truth. "Be diligent to present yourself approved to God as a workman who does not need to be ashamed, accurately handling the word of truth" (2 Timothy 2:15 NASB).

"You shall know the truth and the truth shall set you free" (John 8:32 KJV).

"For the LORD is good; his mercy is everlasting; and his truth endures to all generations" (Psalm 100:5 KJV).

Prayer: Lord, we thank you for your truth, protection, and blessings.

THE LORD IS MY ROCK

"The Lord is my rock, my light and my salvation. In him will I fear and put my trust" (Psalm 18 KJV).

It is an awesome sight when we can see God's majesty at work

I HAVE FLOWN THE CHICAGO to Seattle jet airways at least a hundred times. Some forty miles southeast of Seattle stands Mount Rainier in its sublime, snow-covered majesty. It looms 14,000 feet high and almost a mile higher than our initial procedure altitude.

This huge rock is just a few miles off the centerline of the airway. It glitters. It is an awesome sight in sunlight when clouds and rain do not obscure the terrain. Mt. Rainier can be seen two hundred miles away in our front windshield. It is an

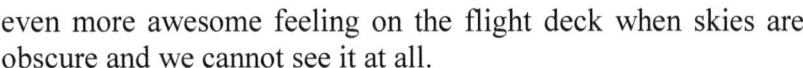

even more awesome feeling on the flight deck when skies are obscure and we cannot see it at all.

If we turn on the weather radar, this rock mountain displays itself like an unchanging, unmoving thunderstorm return. In restricted visibilities we are even more on our toes flying as precisely as our instruments will allow. These are the times we trust our instruments and use backup systems. Moreover, a well-seasoned flight crew is an added bonus.

Spiritually, when we cannot see our way, we must put our trust in God's precise Word and promises. His Word will guide us safely around the mountains in our lives.

It is an awesome sight when we can see God's majesty at work. However, when our vision is restricted and we see through a glass darkly, the same well-seasoned Word and promises keep us safe from harm. He is our Captain.

Conventional wisdom tells us what we should trust. However, we are not to be conventional Christians. We are to be Spirit-filled Christians. "The Lord is our rock and our salvation. In him we will fear and put our trust."

"Do not tremble, do not be afraid. Did I not proclaim this and foretell it long ago? You are my witnesses. Is there any God besides me? No, there is no other Rock; I know not one" (Isaiah 44:8 NIV).

MUSEUM RELICS

THERE IS A BOEING 727 display at the Chicago Science and Industry Museum. It is aircraft number 7003, the first 727 flown in commercial passenger service. I have flown this aircraft hundreds of times. When it was retired out of service, it was flown to the museum, not trucked in. Then it was repainted in its original colors. Someday I will take my grandchildren to see it and reminisce with me. I can hear them now, "Wow, Granddad! You flew that?"

"Yes! Once at forty-two thousand feet" I will say. "Airplanes were not created to be museum pieces."

Airplanes are not to stay at airport gates either. Anytime an airliner parks at the gate, ramp, or taxiway, it is doing what it cannot do for long without damage to the bottom line of the airline. It must be flying. "I am come that they might have life, and have it more abundantly" (John 10:10 NASB).

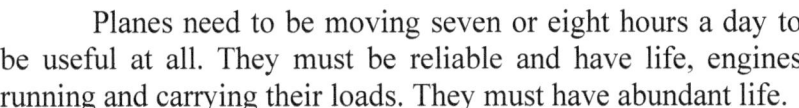

Planes need to be moving seven or eight hours a day to be useful at all. They must be reliable and have life, engines running and carrying their loads. They must have abundant life.

Christians are saved to new life and abundant life. Then he who sat on the throne said, "Behold, I make all things new" (Revelation 21:5 KJV). The old life is gone and behold, all things are made new.

Pilots do not build aircraft, but they enter them to light the fires, activate the hydraulics, carry the flying community, and put planes into service. "I have come that you might have life" (John 10:10 KJV).

Christians do not build the kingdom of God but enter it in service for the community of the saints and the sinners. They do not dwell outside of fellowship but carry their load, living the life of service. Do not be a museum Christian. When they take you out of service, let them "truck you in."

WHERE ARE WE?

WHEN WE WERE SMALL CHILDREN, we asked repeatedly, "Where are we?" "Where are we going now?" and "Are we there yet?" Time, to us, was the present, and we were still learning patience.

As adults, maybe those questions should be of paramount importance. It is for sure we are getting there now, and the time is short.

Often while enroute, airline pilots get a call from a flight attendant. They say, "There's a passenger back here who wants to know where we are."

Our answer in fun sometimes is, "We don't know. We were just trying to figure that out ourselves." And then before the flight attendant can hang up the intercom, we will announce to the cabin our present position and progress of the flight. At least we relieve the monotony of the moment.

There are many ways to know where we are. When flying in CAVU (clear and visibility unlimited conditions) we can look out and see landmarks near and far and recognize cities, lakes, mountains, and structures in every part of the country; for example, Lake Erie or Cleveland, Mt. Rainier, or Ship Rock, etc. We do not fly blind. Our global position systems are accurate within feet.

Another question often asked is, "Are we there yet?" We dislike being delayed enroute by weather and traffic saturation. I can recall many enroute delays from the west coast to Chicago O'Hare when suddenly ATC issues this clearance: "Cleared direct Janesville" (VOR). It is always good news. Monotony is ending and Chicago approach control has accepted us. Get ready for approach and landing.

Likewise, in our spiritual lives we need to know where we are—our present position and current progress. We live in a day of spiritual monotony. It is easy to drift along, encountering delays, mistaking landmarks, and missing signposts in our faith.

C.S. Lewis warns of the gradual road to hell, with gentle slope, and few signposts. However, truly spiritual souls are not blind to the dangers of spiritual monotony. They hear the good news of acceptance and progress toward their eternal goal. And they can cease asking, "Are we there yet?"

So where are we and are we there yet? No, but it is time to get ready for final approach and landing. "Watch therefore: for you know not what hour your Lord is coming" (Matthew 24:42 NJKV).

A FLIGHT DELAY

*We all have a destination, a
future appointment to keep.*

Airplanes were lined along the taxiways and were at a standstill. All inbound flights were being diverted. Thankfully, we were still at the gate when the ground stop was issued at Chicago O'Hare due to severe weather in the area. Traffic was backed up, and I anticipated several hours of delay. Some of our passengers chose to stay in their seats; others wandered up the jet bridge in search of a quick snack.

As the captain and I sat on the flight deck, without introduction he picked up our conversation from last evening's dinner.

"Christianity may be true for you, but it isn't true for me. No religion can be universal. What's right for you isn't necessarily right for me. I believe truth is relative and depends on who you are and how you process it. There are no absolutes."

I responded to him, "Christianity teaches that we are all on a journey…that all of creation has a shelf life. This world will pass away. Even the meals in our galley have a shelf life. For example, if we are delayed more that three or four hours, we probably cannot serve those meals."

I continued. "Now, the people sitting back there waiting are probably wondering if they will reach their destinations tonight. Some passengers will decide not to go at all and will get off the airplane. But for sure, one hundred percent of us will keep our appointments in the future."

The captain smiled at me. "You just proved my point," he said. "It's all relative. There are no absolutes."

We continued our friendly but serious conversation.

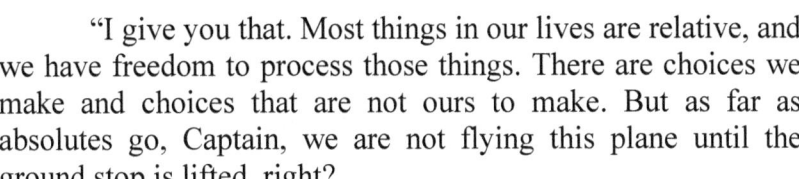

"I give you that. Most things in our lives are relative, and we have freedom to process those things. There are choices we make and choices that are not ours to make. But as far as absolutes go, Captain, we are not flying this plane until the ground stop is lifted, right?

"And think about this: Right now as we sit at the gate, no flight forces are operating on this airplane. But once we get airborne, there will be some absolute laws of physics working on this airframe that we will absolutely have to deal with. As a matter of necessity for the duration of flight, you will become a believer in absolutes."

We all have a destination. Christianity is the eschatological faith that teaches all of God's creation have a future appointment to keep. "And as it is appointed for men to die once, but after this the judgment" (Hebrews 9:27 NKJV); "For God so loved the world, that he gave his only begotten Son, that whosoever believeth in him, should not perish, but have everlasting life" (John 3:16 KJV).

THE CENTERLINE

AIRLINE PILOTS HAVE A GREAT affinity for the taxiway centerline. In fact, the centerline defines the pilot.

Look out the window at your next departure gate. If the airplane nosewheel is not squarely parked on the centerline, it's a pilot disgrace. If you are not on the centerline, all other things don't fit right (like the jet bridge, loading equipment, and other adjacent airplanes).

Staying on the centerline of the taxiway is necessary for safe clearance of boundaries and obstacles. Otherwise, it's a sure way to end up in the mud. Sloppy and imprecise taxiing simply does not have a place in the pilot's life.

The centerline is a visual thing. Although the pilot cannot see his nosewheel, he knows when he on the centerline. Precise taxi is a skill to which all pilots are committed. At night,

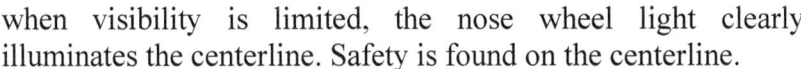

when visibility is limited, the nose wheel light clearly illuminates the centerline. Safety is found on the centerline.

Most importantly, landing on the centerline of the landing runway is the number-one indication that shows the pilot's ability to control the aircraft rather than the crosswind currents taking control of the pilot.

Our nation has socially, financially, and spiritually departed the centerline. We now face a new social and economic paradigm because of gross corruption, greed, and dark evils, which we have not addressed. This event has served only to further delay and obscure our unresolved sins for which we must eventually give account. These sins include abortion, seekers of pleasure, materialism, the love of money, and other idolatries. We must repent.

The new paradigm in which we now face is akin to newly constructed taxiways, which do not yet have the safety benefit of a centerline. This paradigm was spoken about by the Apostle Paul when he wrote, "For we wrestle not against flesh and blood, but against principalities, against powers, against the rulers of the darkness of this world, against spiritual wickedness in high places" (Ephesians 5:12 KJV).

The centerline is where we will individually find God's will. A holy life is the only real evidence that we have a saving faith in Jesus Christ.

We may not know the bottom of the stock market; we sometimes cannot see daylight for
the darkness of life's situations, but we can know where God's centerline takes us. Navigating the centerline is not legalism. The centerline is where we will individually find God's will.

Do not let crosscurrents change your approach. Live your life on the centerline, and you will avoid lurking trouble and not get mired up in mud. God will do the rest. A holy life is the only real evidence that we have a saving faith in Jesus Christ, and the centerline is the holy way.

The warning continues from the Apostle Paul: "Awake, you who sleep, arise from the dead, and Christ will give you light" (Ephesians 5:14 NJKV); "Whoever claims to live in Him must walk as Jesus walked" (Ephesians 5:14 NKJV).

MY BROTHER'S KEEPER

EVERY YEAR WE HAVE ABOUT a dozen results of positive drug-alcohol tests on flight crewmembers. These surprise tests can be conducted immediately before or after a flight. Recently we had yet another pilot deciding he was above the law, attempting to work a scheduled flight from Heathrow to Chicago. No doubt, this was not the first time this pilot erred. A breathalyzer test was ordered on a tip from a concerned and right- thinking crewmember. He failed that test.

God asked Cain: "Where is your brother? 'Am I my brother's keeper?'" Cain asked God (Genesis 4:9 KJV). His words emphasize people's hesitation to accept responsibility for the welfare of their fellow man. However, Christianity teaches that we do have this responsibility. In this case, it is not only a moral but a legal responsibility.

Our lives have a centerline. Better still, we know when we are on it. However, it is easy for the centerline not to be that important to us. We let self and ego sometimes blur our vision, and we fail to track it. Our spouses and best friends see those attitudes first.

We are our brother's keeper for our families' sake. Sometimes our friends and fellow workers do not hold us accountable. The hammer of justice will fall, sometimes with unneeded tragedy.

Thankfully, this fellow crewmember knew his moral responsibility. Am I my brother's keeper? Yes. We all occupy a seat in the cabin, and we journey together. The centerline is our protection. Keep your brother in mind.

CHAIN OF EVENTS

"The steps of a righteous man are ordered by the Lord and he delights in his way" (Psalm 37:23 NJKV).

Our Christian journey is a chain of events tied to each other in obedience.

IN 1972 A DOUGLAS L 1011 airplane crashed in a slow descent into the everglades eleven miles short of Miami's runway 9 left. A burned-out bulb that indicated an unsafe landing gear in the nosewheel well started this chain of events that led to the total loss of hull and life of that flight.

This crew did not lack the ability to fly but failed to fly the airplane, a sin of omission. It was wrong thinking. The crew was in consensus on the problem, but no one noticed the disconnected autopilot. The jumbo jet slowly settled from 1,500 feet into the swamp while the three pilots tried to determine if the landing gear was fully down, simply because a tiny light bulb did not illuminate. This accident was a chain of events that included wrong thinking by three highly trained, experienced pilots.

Likewise, failure in the Christian life is almost never a single omission. It is wrong thinking, consensus thinking, focusing on the wrong thing, the wrong person.

In the same way, a cloudy mixing of religious beliefs has invaded our bookstores and churches. Reincarnation, karma, fortune telling, and pantheism are widespread among some churchgoers. Transcendental meditation is not new but has swept the United States as a remedy for human failings and societal ills, leaving a trail of events, a departure from the truth.

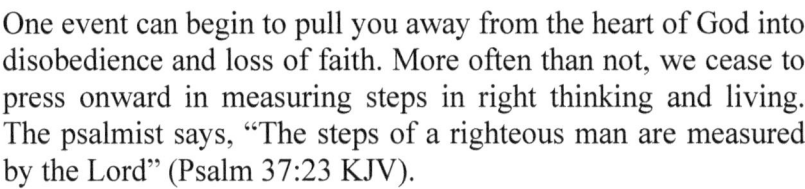

One event can begin to pull you away from the heart of God into disobedience and loss of faith. More often than not, we cease to press onward in measuring steps in right thinking and living. The psalmist says, "The steps of a righteous man are measured by the Lord" (Psalm 37:23 KJV).

A single event almost never causes an aviation accident. It is a chain of events of which the first event is unseen or unchecked. Then Murphy's Law takes over. You recall the complete meaning of Murphy's Law: "If anything can go wrong, it will, and at the most inopportune time."

Our Christian journey is a chain of events tied to each other in obedience, sometimes without decisive clarity but still in faith and purpose. The Lord delights in every detail of our lives, so keep measuring your every step. Keep walking.

GOD'S HIGHER POWER

DEPARTING DENVER INTERNATIONAL AIRPORT, A pilot could likely hear this clearance from ATC (Air Traffic Control): "United 324, cleared as filed, fly heading zero-niner-five, Goodland transition, maintain niner thousand. You have traffic, eleven o'clock, descending to one-three thousand; additional VFR crossing traffic at ten thousand five hundred. Expect higher in twenty miles. Read back."

What does this mean to the pilot? Simply this: You can expect to fly your flight plan to destination with some restrictions. We are protecting you from opposing traffic until you have a clear corridor. Expect higher altitudes after the conflict passes. ATC will keep you from endangering airplanes and clear of other traffic. Read back and stay with us.

Likewise, our Christian lives must stay under the auspice of the Controller of the skies. He knows the dangers and gives his guidance and wisdom. "For as many who are led by the Spirit of God, they are the sons of God… The Spirit itself bears witness with our spirit that we are the children of God" (Romans 8:14-16 KJV).

Christians live under the guidance of the Holy Spirit, but our maturity in the Christian life is not automatic. We must trust the resources God gives us. "If God be for us, who can be against us" (Romans 8:31 KJV).

With God, we are cleared to a higher plane. Have a great flight!

THE NEED FOR HIGH FLIGHT

AIRLINE PILOTS NEVER FEEL THEY are on their way to destination until they receive clearance to higher altitudes. At low altitudes, range is limited because fuel resources burn at an alarming rate. An airliner might sustain flight only for three hours at 8,000 feet when it could sustain a six-hour flight at 35,000 thousand feet, covering five times greater distance, using the same amount of fuel. In the same manner, the space shuttle main fuel tanks must be jettisoned after a few minutes if the shuttle has any chance for its destination in orbit.

    The Christian life is like this. What do we need to jettison to sustain flight at higher spiritual altitudes? We do not have the resources to go far on our own power. We can only realize God's sustaining power when we live on God's higher plane. "Now glory be to God who by his mighty power at work within us is able to do far more than we could ever dare to dream of, infinitely beyond our highest thoughts, prayers, desires or hopes" (Ephesians 3:20 TLB).

There is a strange and wonderful thing about being dependent on God!

We do not go far in the spiritual kingdom on our own limitations. We are designed for God's higher plane. The gospel hymn writer Reverent Johnson Oatman wrote these words:

> I'm pressing on the upward way; new heights I'm gaining every day.
>
> Still praying as I onward bound, Lord, plant my feet on higher ground.
>
> I want to scale the utmost height and catch a gleam of glory bright.
>
> But still I'll pray till heaven I've found. Lord, lead me on to higher ground.
>
> Lord lift me up, and let me stand, by faith on Heaven's tableland.
>
> A higher plane than I have found, Lord, lead me on to higher ground.

There is a strange and wonderful thing about being dependent on God and it is this: the more we are, the more wonderful it is! And it is because of this reason: the gospel of Christ is not mere philosophy. It is not theory. It is a relationship. Only the power of the Holy Spirit can enable us to run the race set before us. With his power, we can soar to God's higher plane. "The Gospel is the power of God unto our salvation" (Romans 1:16 KJV).

AGENDAS AND HOAXES

*Sincerity and agendas tend to give
credibility and veracity to one's belief
even in the face of contrary evidence.*

ON NOVEMBER 7, 2006, SOME of my flying friends at O'Hare International Airport saw a UFO, or Unidentified Aerial Phenomena, the new, preferred term. Dozens of employees observed this craft at 4:30 p.m. hovering in daylight over United Gate 17 as a Boeing 777 aircraft was being pushed off the gate. It appeared to be six to twenty-four feet long before it rapidly disappeared in the gray, 1,900-foot overcast sky. Air traffic controllers observed nothing, nor did the radar show any image returns. (Maybe it was God's mirror in the skies.)

A few tower controllers made jokes at the report, while some employees were upset that the government did not investigate. Observations like these easily create agendas or hoaxes and often lead to the loss of objectivity.

The Roswell UFO sightings of 1947 generated fervent believers and hoaxes. They still persist today. UFOs are exciting because they are unidentified. We still live in a day of agendas and hoaxes. Sincerity and agendas tend to give credibility and veracity to one's belief even in the face of contrary evidence. The O.J. Simpson trial in 1995 is an example. Each decade seems to breed some urgent hysteria that gains momentum.

The Sadducees disbelieved in a resurrected body. They considered it a hoax, and their agenda was to oppose anyone who did believe. However, Jesus's bodily resurrection was prophesied, and the news of it spread like wildfire. First Corinthians 1:14 claims that Jesus appeared to more than five hundred people shortly after his resurrection, but it did not deter the religious leaders' agenda to disavow the obvious truth.

Every period of history has had its agendas and hoaxes. The present global warming debate is only one of many controversies while theories are sorted out from fact. With the passing of time, agendas and hoaxes will fall away while truth and God's Word will remain. "Heaven and earth shall pass away, but my words shall not pass away" (Luke 21:33 NAS). God's account of creation will occur on his schedule, not ours.

PART THREE

MAKING ADJUSTMENTS

SHORTLY AFTER I GOT ON the flying line, after initial training, I realized that I had a big adjustment to make if I would be a successful airline pilot. The captain's words hit me like a ton of bricks:

> Quit analyzing your engineer panel back there and become a part of my flight team up here. Get engaged up front. You are a hundred miles behind the airplane. Get your eyes outside and look for aircraft. Get into the loop, and you'll think like a captain. The airplane is not going to fall out of the sky, so there's no need to stare at your panel.

The words really stung.

I was a new hire second officer, a flight engineer. I knew my systems well, but I knew I was not pleasing the boss. My perfection as a flight engineer meant nothing to him. I had to be an active part of the crew. I had to get into the loop as if I were at the controls.

As a musician and performer, I was a perfectionist and had trained and managed hundreds of fine volunteers. However, I quickly realized that my cockpit interaction with fellow crewmembers would involve hands-on accountability and backing them up with flight info.

The fog outside the windshield had become a fog in my mind. I not only needed to know my job but also how to evaluate the captain and first officer duties to make them successful and keep them out of trouble.

The captain later told me, "Within a year or two, you'll be sitting up here flying. I could be riding in your airplane with

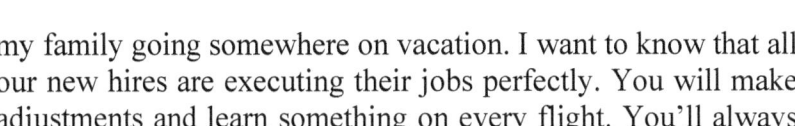

my family going somewhere on vacation. I want to know that all our new hires are executing their jobs perfectly. You will make adjustments and learn something on every flight. You'll always be a student of flying."

It was a good adjustment, one that I would put into practice.

Seeing another point of view is a valuable and indeed cheap education.

My parents taught me to be a student of life. Growing up with other siblings in our family, I had to learn to share in the process of give and take. Whatever the method, our happiness and motivation increases and greater success is possible as we accept responsibility for our own actions while listening to the advice of others.

I'm not sure when we begin to learn how to make adjustments in our attitudes and expectations of people in our life, but I am convinced that life gets easier when we learn that things don't always have to go our way. Flexibility is always a good thing, both in bones and brain matter. We can avoid a lot of bruises and broken bones by listening. Moreover, seeing another point of view is a valuable and indeed cheap education.

Understanding personality types on the flight deck enables better communication.
Strong-personality captains do better when their captain's authority is diplomatic. On the other hand, a passive captain must step up to the plate with strong, commanding leadership to build confidence in teamwork.

A healthy case of skepticism with guarded diplomacy in flight is just about the right adjustment. Rigidity of mindset can bring unnecessary strife and relational problems in the workplace. While airline pilots must adhere to checklists and procedures, a rigid approach can cause blind spots and lack of perception. "Adjusting" is the operative word.

\

ABRUPTNESS

HOW ABRUPT ARE YOUR WORDS? How abrupt is your spirit? Do you often speak too hastily, too haughty in pride, not measuring your words? Is it lack of trust? Is it unbelief?

The airline pilot is always looking for that perfect flight where there are no abrupt turns, surprises, hurry-up maneuvers, loss of situational awareness, or lack of communication. A "good flight" is when the passengers do not notice anything but a smooth, dreamy flight from gate to gate without abrupt turns or G forces...the kind of flight on which you can snooze.

I recall several times that an air traffic controller issued a command saying, "United 553, traffic twelve o'clock four miles, give me a hard left turn immediately to zero one zero degrees."

Our immediate response is to believe and obey. In those cases, we execute immediately and apologize to the passengers later. Abruptness on the controls at the speed we fly is no fun for the crew or passengers. We all like easy, measured turns.

Likewise, our words we speak should be measured and not abrupt. We live in a day when public courtesies are ebbing low. We push our way into airplanes and elevators and lose situational awareness of others around us. This spills over into our family life and common friendships. Yet a gentle spirit and kind words are lovely to hear. We need to slow down, stay in our airspace, measure our words, sweeten them, and relearn courtesies of our grandparents and believe.

How abrupt are your words? How abrupt is your spirit? "Those things which proceed out of the mouth, come from the heart, and they defile a man" (Matthew 15:18 NASB). These words of Jesus described and irritated the Pharisees because of their pride and unbelief.

If you hold a cup of liquid in your hand and someone vigorously shakes your arm, someone will get wet. Whenever we are irritated, whatever is in our cup will come spilling out.
This is what Jesus meant when he said, "Those things which proceed out of the mouth, come from the heart, and they defile a man." No one can provoke what is not inside you. "A merry heart doeth good like medicine, but a broken spirit dries the bones" (Proverbs 17:22 KJV).

*The flight deck of our lives is our
place of learning as well as doing.*

Likewise, the words we speak should be measured, like good medicine, and not abrupt.
Our words are not all that defile us. Our attitudes, our spirits, and our body language all contribute to an atmosphere that can become contagious or become a hindrance.
The flight deck of our lives is our place of learning as well as doing. Our spiritual need requires a deeper cleansing than we can do ourselves. We can decide to "turn over a new leaf," and we should. We can change our use of words, measure them out, and sweeten them with patience and praise—and we should. We can hold our tongue and simmer in anger—and we should. But every human heart needs a deeper cleansing than we can do ourselves. God's Holy Spirit needs to dwell in us. We must ask him to take control of our spirit and our lives—and believe. "Humble yourselves in the sight of the Lord and he shall lift you up" (James 4:10 KJV).
We generally dislike proud and arrogant people who strut and brag about their achievements, while we admire those who are humble. Jesus said the meek shall inherit the earth, and C.S. Lewis reminds us that "pride" is the greatest sin. We easily see faults in others, and we tend to enjoy the spotlight until it reveals our own shortcomings and deficiencies.

SO HOW DO YOU FLY AN AIRPLANE?

SEVERAL YEARS AGO ON A long transcontinental flight, the flight attendant, Nancy, came up to the flight deck for a third time. She said as she sat on the edge of the forward jump seat, "We are so busy back there; I just need another break. You know, every time I come into the cockpit, it looks like you guys are just sitting here doing nothing."

I said, "Yes, Nancy, and that's the way you really prefer it because if it ever looks like we are busy up here and things are moving in the windshield, or we've got our flight books out talking to each other, or not drinking coffee…by the way, could I have a black?"

"Sure. Don't go anywhere. I'll be right back."…

"Thanks! Oh, that smells good! As I was saying, if anything is moving like bank, pitch, or ground coming up, then we want everything to slow down real fast, back to nothing moving. Our job is to look like we've doing nothing!"

"Oh, I bet I can do that!" She laughed.

So that's the way you fly, I tell my students. If anything is happening too fast, your job is to make all of it slow down. That includes your muscles, movement of flight controls, instruments, and objects in the windshield. Good flying is effortless, no tension. It is relaxing in your seat. That's the way you do almost anything well. Get it done smoothly and relax.

I once had an unnamed student (a good friend) who was too relaxed for me in his primary flight lessons. He held the flight controls with one thumb, not the entire hand, and he talked (as in conversation) on takeoff. He was an excellent "stick." He had the gist of flying naturally. After three lessons, he could have taken the airplane around the pattern by himself. However, learning to fly is ninety percent bookwork…attitude adjustment!

You learn to fly until you retire.

HELP FOR THE JOURNEY

PRIOR TO CHANGING FREQUENCIES, PILOTS sometimes tell air traffic controllers, "Thanks for your help." Likewise when a pilot makes a timely maneuver to accommodate other air traffic, the controller will say to the pilot, "Nice job." You see, we really have to work together when traffic conflicts arise.

Some flights demand altitudes with strong tailwinds to stretch the fuel burn, so a fuel stop is not required. However, en-route weather can limit the altitude or the load we can carry. Traffic conflicts and turbulence may also limit the desirable altitudes as well.

I remember a flight from Cleveland to Seattle. With our load and strong headwinds that day, we had to plan a contingency fuel stop at Des Moines in order to arrive with legal fuel. However, the next week, the same flight did not require fuel contingency planning.

Easterly flights generally have a tailwind. Conversely, westerly flights most often encounter headwinds and flight distances are limited. Perhaps you are aware of someone facing a "headwind" in their life right now.

We often need help for the journey, perhaps a fuel stop or reducing our load. We don't always see the contingencies of life that might await us.

Likewise, as Christian friends, we also need to encourage each other when facing the headwinds of life. True friends can help each other to be accountable to the important decisions that must be made along the way.

We are more blessed in Christian fellowship than we sometimes know. Our relationship with God is unique from all other faiths. Atheist Madalyn Murray O'Hair accused Christians as needing a "crutch." It is not a crutch! We know it as a relationship in Christ. How blessed we are!

"And the Holy Spirit helps us in our weakness. For example, we don't know sometimes how to pray. But the Holy Spirit prays for us with groanings that cannot be expressed in words" Romans 8:26 (NLB).

We do have help for the journey.

THE SCHOOL ANSWER

Relationships are always more challenging than rules.

AIRLINE PILOTS MUST UNDERSTAND THE school answer for everything when they attend their annual training and upgrades. However, they also realize they have to execute the flight procedure in the real world when flying the line. You can only simulate so much.

Airline pilots know that flying the line involves trusting relationships with their flight crew and the ever-changing demands of flight. Relationships are always more challenging than rules. Rules try to control you, give you knowledge, but relationships can save your life.

Such is the case with United Flight 232 that crash landed with a total hydraulic failure in Sioux Falls in July 1989 after the center engine hub blew apart. The flight controls were disabled, leaving the DC-10 with no steering and forcing the flight crew to invent procedures never before done in an airplane.

According to Captain Al Haynes, he and his flight officers were successful only because of the strong trusting community that the entire flight crew demonstrated during that emergency. There were no school answers to that dilemma.

Denny Fitch, a United Airlines training instructor, was deadheading on that doomed flight and offered his help. Captain Haynes asked Captain Fitch to join the flight crew as they used timed alternate throttle settings as their sole directional control to get in position for a zero flight control, no brake, and no flap landing at 215 mph on a 6,000-foot closed runway.

They were descending at thirty feet per second in an aircraft that could only manage right turns. Yet 186 souls lived to walk out of Iowa cornfields because of an aviation community that believed in living answer relationships.

Captain Fitch was my flying comrade many times after that fateful flight. We had many hours of believer-to-believer conversations. He described to me how God changed his life and led him into truth and relationship with the Holy Spirit that he had never experienced before.

Phillip P. Young, in his novel *The Shack*, discusses religious answers versus the Living Answer. He says:

> Religion is about having the right answers, and some of their answers are right. But (God) is about the process that takes you to the living answer and once you get to Him, He will change you from the inside.
>
> (p.198, The Shack; Windblown Media; windblownmedia.com)

God is the Living Answer.

God is the Living Answer. He wants a relationship with us. Simply knowing the school answer without trusting him is futile. From the very beginning, God pursues an everlasting relationship with us.

Novelist Young further says:

> There are a lot of smart people who are able to say a lot about the right answers from their brain because they have been told what the right answers are, but they don't know (God) at all. So how can they be right even if they are right?"
>
> The Shack; Windblown Media; windblownmedia.com

In John Chapter 16, Jesus taught his disciples many things to keep them from stumbling. He promised them the Holy Spirit would lead them into all truth concerning the mysteries of the Kingdom of God.

The Bible (the school answer) will redirect you to where you can develop the right relationship with God's Holy Spirit.

The Living Word will lead you to truth. The difference is in knowing the truth and living in the truth. "When He, the Holy Spirit is come, He will lead you into all Truth" (John 13:16 TNIV).

GOING THROUGH THE MOTIONS

YOU ARE A RARE PERSON indeed if you've never "just marked time." But on the other hand, if you have ever felt that you are just "going through the motions" for any length of time, then welcome to the human race. But therein lays the inherent danger.

There are two dangers a pilot faces in the cockpit.

> One: Letting events get out of the normal flow.
>
> Two: Just going through the motions of flying.

Add just one surprise event, and you've got a full-blown emergency. A good captain will avoid these two dangers

An example of this on the world grand scheme, need I say, is 9/11.

An experienced captain develops an advanced skill. It might even be called a sixth sense, one of sensing lethargy or uncertainty, and avoiding situations that could lead away from normal flight operations.

"What does it take to be a captain, anyway?" That's a fun, mocking question first officers sometimes ask their captain when he makes an astute decision that changes the flow of events that later proves timely and correct.

It could even be the first officer who responsibly changes the flow to keep the flight on target. Someone must be willing to speak up and challenge the moment.

Case in point: I relate a procedural mistake our flight crew made one morning at six a.m., one that I never repeated. We were good friends and we trusted each other. Here's the flow of events that morning:

We were holding short of the takeoff runway; the tower cleared us into position to hold. As the captain swung the nose of the aircraft around to runway heading he said to me, "Your airplane!" Then as he flipped on the exterior lights and strobe, he said, "Runway heading to 5000, brakes released."
The second officer said, "Takeoff check complete." I pushed the throttles up to close the bleed air valves to start the takeoff roll.
As we started the roll I said, "Cleared for takeoff." It was then that I queried the tower. "Are we cleared for takeoff?"
"Negative, but you are cleared now to fly heading three-one-zero after takeoff, maintain five thousand, cleared for takeoff."

We had almost taken off without clearance. Classify it as going through the motions. Classify it as a brush with danger and certainly an impending procedural violation.
It was a big deal. We got the procedure right but got ahead of ourselves on our checklist. You can be sure we performed perfect flying the rest of that day!

After we got squared away at cruise altitude, we reviewed the flow of events.

We should not have completed our callouts until the tower had clearly said, "Cleared for takeoff." The brakes should have been set, requiring me to release them rather than holding them manually. Adherence to procedure is important.

Our friendship had failed to hold us accountable to strict procedure that morning. It's a mistake we can easily make in our lives and relationships with people who trust us.

In a very basic sense, it is "just going through the motions."

Today we face worldwide moral, ethical, and survival issues on a scale perhaps never before seen in history. Remaining silent and hands off is not an option. We can no longer mark time. Worldwide terrorism, nuclear threat, and economic collapse are real possibilities. Abnormal times call for an end of going through the motions.

We need clarity of mind and plenty of fuel.

FLIRTING WITH THE RUNWAY

We live in an enticing and seductive world. It calls to us and distracts us.

"You are cleared for a visual approach." Sounds like wonderful words to an airline pilot. Visual approaches are fun to do. They test our skills but contain inherent implications and dangers. The fact is that visual approaches present much greater latitude for error because it is a shortcut.

However, the upside is, "Good! I can conduct this visual approach my way, bypass the outer marker, and land quicker without restrictions from the tower." The downside is the tower ceases to give pertinent information like traffic separation or unforeseen conflicts and the pilot's judgment becomes more critical. The flight crew accepts this liability when they receive a clearance for a visual approach. Instrument pilots must master two disciplines—instrument flight rules (IFR) and visual flight rules (VFR)—because they fly in both flight conditions.

Our Christian living must endure the spiritual world and the visual world. When we live in God's Spirit, we live by faith. When we live in the visual world, we can get distracted and live by sight. John 17:15: "My prayer is not that you take them out of the world but that you protect them from the evil one" (NIV). Christians live in an enticing and seductive world. It calls us and distracts us. We must master two disciplines. We are to be in the world but not of the world. We were once broken but now empowered by the Spirit and cleared to land in a visual broken, distracted world, to be witnesses of Jesus to those who are fallen and frightened.

A clear weather (VFR Pilot) is useless in airline flying and cannot fly without an instrument rating. Flying in the "soup" must be practiced and kept current to be of any use at all. Likewise, we must be practice our Christian life and keep our faith current to be of any use to a world that only lives by sight. Otherwise, we become distracted to live like our godless culture.

My analogy is this: the world is our runway and God is our outer marker. We flirt with the world every day. Our spiritual lives are much like our approaches to the touchdown zone. An instrument approach is precise and begins at the outer marker where we connect with the glide slope.

However, visual approaches give many more choices, and those choices can make for "loosey goosey" flirting with the runway. A visual approach is a riddle to be solved early in the approach. It can look and feel like trouble. Only advanced pilots can do them precisely.

We flirt with the world every day. God is our "outer marker." Use the outer marker.
It is our safest approach. It is precise living. "I will keep Thy precepts with my whole heart" (Psalm 119:69 KJV).

CONSENSUS OR CHECKLIST?

AIRPLANES ARE NOT FLOWN CASUALLY or by consensus but by extensive checklists. The captain is in charge of the final decisions and the flight crew and must practice a healthy pessimism on the flight deck. They need not be antagonistic or negative. They may even be friendly but never casual. They are checklist driven.

When I was a new first officer, I was deeply impressed by the doubtful approach of my captain to anything that came along slightly off the beaten track of normalcy. By this, I judged his experience level.

When I became a captain, I briefed my flight crew that we expected to have fun, enjoy our flying, but we would never be casual in out flight duties. I was on guard against a casual attitude or neglect of checklists.

Religious truth is not by consensus.

Sometimes we take our religion too casually. But we aren't casual in the business world. Our postmodern mood blurs the truth and we get careless. The twenty-first-century church tries to be relevant and often becomes pluralistic. We attack religiosity and we become judgmental. We try not to be too theological, and clarity of the Christian message suffers.

We pilots are mission oriented and must deal with what is relevant to completing a flight. In other words, knowing and judging what is relevant. While we are mission oriented, we have to know when certainty is a myth.

For example, flying from airport A to airport B is the mission. But that is also the myth. It may be necessary to fly to airport C to avoid violating legalities, the operating manual, for safety, or the FAA certificate, etc. This is the real mission.

Aviation is governed by international civil law, but a legal airplane can still be an unknown quantity with inherent risks in flying. Pilots have to bring the unknown to the known and make a judgment. We Christians must bring our unknown to the known, to the eternal God of all knowledge. It is not difficult.

My point is this: religious truth is not by consensus. One of my favorite teenage manipulations of my parents was, "Everybody's got one, everybody is going, and everybody is doing it," to which the reply was, "That has no bearing on what you will or can do." Independent living did not exist at my house.

In the Old Testament, the Israelites, by consensus, demanded a king like other nations. Prophets and Judges were not enough. Consensus is always popular because it seems so relevant. I once heard a minister say, "A church is not a democratic body or a business. Nor does a church board govern by representation but by mission decisions."

This is our mission: to discern truth as faithful believers of our communities and followers of Christ. The mission is not just point A to point B. We must make judgments that are not popular. We must examine consensus with reality, the truth of God's Word, and experience. This path will keep us on mission in our lives and our churches.

Question: What is our mission in life? Are we on target?

FLYING BY FAITH

PILOTS FLY BY FAITH MUCH of the time, not by sight. We do not have to see the entire picture; we just have faith in the part we cannot see. For example, we know on a foggy landing that each runway edge light is spaced every two hundred feet apart.

In Category 2 operations we are legal to land if we see six lights—twelve hundred-feet RVR (runway visual range); that is not much at 140 miles per hour! We do not have to see the whole picture, but we see by faith the whole picture. If we fly precisely, our flight instruments give us faith in the part we cannot see.

When we drive our cars on foggy nights, we exercise this same kind of faith. We do not have to see all the stoplights or streetlights, but we trust by faith that they will come into sight as we need them. We can drive all the way home even on foggy nights. We do not have to see the entire picture but by faith, trust the picture to come into focus as we make decisions.

By faith, Abraham started a long journey that God commanded. He had no idea of the picture God had framed for him. Yet he started. He was obedient.

Airline pilots often ask themselves this funny question: "Why are we checking the weather? We're going to fly anyway, aren't we?" Yes, and we jokingly say we need to know how scared we should be as we exercise our faith.

When flying a low-visibility approach, we call it "taking a look." This is why in our spiritual lives we should always get started without seeing the entire picture. Yet often we want to see the whole picture before we begin; in other words, before we exercise our faith. We say, "Lord, just show me the picture, and I will do it." However, that is not faith at all.

Prayer: Lord, give us faith to get started. Give us the faith of airline pilots. Give us the faith of Abraham...the faith to get started. Amen.

COMMUNICATIONS

US AVIATION EXPERIENCED A SHORT but massive communication failure. A vital link that transmitted flight clearances failed. Airplanes could not takeoff or land at most cities east of Cleveland and Atlanta. Due to the ripple effect, hundreds of flights all across the North American air route system were canceled. The failure was a main communication center located at an undisclosed location south of Atlanta. The ability to issue flight clearances was lost. Control towers, flight clearance, ground control, departure control, and regional centers had no information and authority to issue clearances for flight. The North American air route system simply shut down.

Flights and clearances must work together. Airspace centers around the nation depend on a communication link without which they have no authority. The Holy Spirit is the vital link for the church. Without him, we have a massive communication failure. A prominent pastor and author recently raised this startling question: "Is the Holy Spirit withdrawing from churches of North America?" Is the Holy Spirit saying to the churches, "Return to me, or have it your way?"

> The Holy Spirit is the vital
> link for the church.

"Remember, therefore, what you have received and heard; obey it, and repent. But if you do not wake up, I will come like a thief, and you will not know at what time I will come to you" (Revelation 3:1-3 NIV). The Holy Spirit leads us into all truth. We must not quench or grieve the Holy Spirit. The church exists only on the vital link of the Holy Spirit.

DEFERRED, BROKEN, OR SHATTERED

A myriad of reasons can cause an airplane to be late and off schedule. It may be that an instrument has failed or a part in a flight system needs to be deferred before departure. So the next time you fly, think of this: It takes thousands of parts and components on an airliner working together in concert with flight systems to make flying from point A to point B possible, safe, and timely. Most flights depart with several deferred items that will be repaired and made new at a later time or on the next scheduled maintenance. You should be comforted knowing that you can takeoff and arrive on schedule with deferred flight items.

And consider this: Airplanes are scheduled for flight in different parts of the world months and even years in advance. In addition, they have maintenance and retirement schedules prepared several years in advance. I have piloted several airplanes on their final revenue flight before being retired to the aircraft bone yard. Most of them had several deferred, broken, or shattered parts.

God defers our faults, schedules our lives in mercy and promises to make all things new.

The same is true for our human condition. We have a schedule. We have imperfect lives. Our lives may be broken and shattered. But God can make us new. He binds the wounds and heals our brokenness. He defers our faults, and he schedules our lives in mercy and love. And he promises to make all things new.

"He who was seated on his (heavenly) throne said, 'I am making everything new!' Then he said, 'Write this down, for these words are trustworthy and true'" (Revelation 21:5 NIV); "Surely he took up our infirmities and carried our sorrows, yet we considered him stricken by God, smitten by him, and afflicted. But he was pierced for our transgressions, he was crushed for our iniquities; the punishment that brought us peace was upon him, and by his wounds we are healed" (Isaiah 53:4-5 NIV).

Christians have a unique and sure hope. Someday we will make that final flight on schedule. And on that glorious day, we will be made whole and complete in Christ.

JUDGING WHAT REALLY MATTERS

"Judge not, lest ye be judged" Matthew 7: 1 (KJV).

"And when you judge, judge righteously" John 7: 1 (KJV).

WE WERE FLYING FROM MIAMI to Chicago...

My pilot friend (Bill from Birmingham) said, "I know people who call themselves Christians, and they are the most judgmental people I know."

"Yes, I replied. That's easy to become a stumbling block to us. We all like to judge each other's behavior and put it on a standard, a morality, if you please. Then we compare ourselves to the standard, right? You do that as well, don't you?"

"Well yes! But I'm not that judgmental," he replied.

I said, "Look, when you land an airplane, you judge where the runway is, right? Well, in the final analysis, the runway judges where you are." You either got it right and made a good landing, or you misjudged it and hid behind the cockpit door when you got to the gate!" I smiled.

Our judgment isn't perfect. The runway is what matters. When we read the Bible, we judge what it says. But in reality, the Word judges us. The Word is what really matters. No one can hide behind the Word in judgment. We must hide the Word in us. God's spirit grows fruit in us. And there is no law for us to judge God's fruit.

God writes his law in our hearts, where it matters.

"The fruit of the Spirit is love, joy, peace, longsuffering, gentleness, goodness, faith, meekness, temperance. Against such, there is no law" (Galatians 5:22-23 KJV).

Bill jumped on that. "Yeah, that law business. That's what I reject. People try to tell me how I ought to live."
I smiled and said, "Bill, God writes his law in our hearts, where it matters. Stop arguing with people and argue with God. That's what matters."

"My parents tried to lay the law down with me about religion when I was a teenager," he replied. "I've not been back to church since then."
"Bill," I continued, "the law is helpless to get us in right fellowship with God. He speaks in our heart with a voice of mercy and love, and it burns because our hearts condemn us. God wants to take away the condemnation and give us a new start, to live in his mercy and forgiveness. We won't suddenly make perfect landings and have perfect judgment, but we can be forgiven and live in God's mercy. That is Christ's love, his mercy for every day. And his mercy is everlasting."

"Renda, we've been flying together all month. Why haven't we talked about this before now." "I really don't know, Bill. I love to talk about my faith in Christ. Our faith is what really matters."

And I felt his words judge me in my failure to be a courageous witness to the open doors he had given previously.

But now it was time to get ready for approach and landing. After all, 150 people were about to judge his landing.

ICING AT LOW ALTITUDES

STRUCTURAL ICING ON AIRPLANES CAN occur rapidly. The added weight and the shape of the airfoil destroy lift, and the margin of safety is suddenly gone. The airplane simply will not fly. Icing conditions existed that afternoon in Butte, Montana, when a Pilatus PC-12 high-end, single-engine turbo prop nose-dived into the ground while on approach. Fourteen children and adults on a skiing trip tragically died.

The pilot spoke to ATC twice about diverting but gave no reason. He apparently descended through an icing layer that may have created possible weight and balance problems.

Flying in freezing rain or freezing drizzle is "strictly prohibited" by FAA regulations. By rule, we cannot continue flight in known icing conditions. Descending through saturated air with temperatures a few degrees below freezing will quickly ice up an airplane. Icing can affect load balance and cause uncertain flight paths and stalls.

The culture of freezing temperatures and saturated moisture is a recipe for icing. Ice adheres on cold aircraft surfaces much like super-cooled droplets on cars and bridges when temperatures are not cold enough to prevent it or warm enough to melt it.

In aviation, we do not experiment with icing. Icing altitudes must be vacated immediately. Pilots do this every day. Look out your window. It is really that simple. We should either climb or descend to colder or warmer air.

Truth mixed with error is more dangerous than outright lies.

Holy Scripture reminds us: "I know your works, that you are neither cold nor hot: I wish you were cold or hot"

(Revelation 3:15 NASB). The Spirit is saying to the churches that truth mixed with error is more dangerous than outright lies, neither cold nor hot. "I will spew you out of my mouth." Meanwhile, as man spews God out of culture, we see alarming and increasing acts of violence. Our culture cannot provide coherent answers for our current dismal estate. With family values and marriage under ferocious attack, our culture lies at an intolerable low altitude of icing. We need to divert back to God before we crash and burn.

Wake up! The greatest opportunity for the Christian church is now before us.

Prayer: Lord, increase our spiritual visibility. Guide us with the clarity of the Gospel. Let us not become lukewarm. Let your Word dwell with and in us. Amen.

SILENCE THE WARNING HORN

I WAS THE SECOND OFFICER. We were on approach for landing. "Gear down, final descent check," commanded the captain. I picked up the checklist and began to read. The landing gear warning horn and a gear unsafe red light indication interrupted me. At that point, we could not confirm that the landing gear was down and locked.

"Silence the warning horn," the captain said curtly. The first officer pushed the horn cutout button, but the loud horn continued to blare. The captain looked at me and said, "Pull the gear warning circuit breaker."

"First, let's execute a missed approach," I said timidly.

"Yes, first things, first! Go-around thrust, positive rate, gear up, check flaps at 15. O'Hare tower, this is United 321, we are breaking off the approach, requesting climb to four thousand," radioed the captain.

As the gear came back up, the warning horn stopped blaring. What a relief of silence! The horn had been so loud we could hardly think. Nevertheless, we were all thinking the same thing now. Follow the book first. We knew we could not just randomly pull circuit breakers without following the checklist procedure.

That "gospel horn" really got my attention! My mind flashed ahead in time. We had fifty-five minutes of usable fuel remaining. Could we safely rescue our flight? Could we get the gear down and locked for landing? Time was of utmost importance.

In retrospect, I knew that a conflict or misalignment in the gear and flaps could cause a warning that could not be silenced. Maybe our problem was simply a faulty position light in the gear-flap system. I hoped we could correct it.

Today, we are tempted to be theologically silenced.

However, I do know this: When it comes to bells and warning horns in the cockpit, silence is golden! We do not like to hear them. Today, we are tempted to be theologically silenced. With America at the secular brink of religious and social disaster, pulpits have largely pulled the circuit breaker, deactivating the warning horn and faulty position light.

Abortion has been the worst godless abomination ever perpetrated by humankind for over thirty-six years. The church is largely silent! There are those among us that say we must be more than one-issue voters! Many of us are timid Christians, hiding our Christian beliefs, pursuing life, while prayer and Bibles are illegal in schools. Gospel sermons could soon be ruled as hate speech. Christian broadcasts could soon be outlawed on public airwaves. Our income taxes could soon be funding abortions.

The church may have been silenced, but the warning horn is sounding loudly. It is hard to think clearly. We must wake up. We cannot be timid. We are in dire need of a go-around procedure. We must break off the approach and face the problem. Political correctness within and without the church would silence the Gospel message. We seem timid and afraid to proclaim the miraculous gospel of Christ, the glories of heaven, and the abhorrence of hell. Gospel "lite" is our fare, sin does not bother us, and the convicting Holy Spirit is grieved. It is we who must be rescued. The gospel horn is powerful when it sounds. We have limited fuel and will land soon. God of all mercy, hear our prayers.

In 1940, Hitler believed the church in Germany to be an empty shell, which with little effort would come crashing down upon itself. It is happening in America. "If my people, who are called by my name, shall humble themselves, and pray, and seek my face, and turn from their wicked ways, I will hear from heaven and will heal their land" (2 Chronicles 7:14 NIV).

DUMPING FUEL

We often find ourselves carrying unnecessary baggage.

HAVE YOU EVER FELT LIKE you need to lighten your load? Although rare, there are times when a pilot needs to dump fuel before landing. It's like getting your house in order. When this occurs, you can be sure flight conditions changed that necessitated the jettisoning of fuel. There are several reasons an aircrew might consider dumping fuel. One example is an unscheduled return for landing.

Similarly, ships, when disabled by a storm, have historically thrown cargo overboard to survive the raging seas. In fact, the Apostle Paul survived just such a shipwreck.

Sometimes we accumulate habits, perceptions, attitudes, or episodes in our lives that simply need to be "dumped" overboard—jettisoned and forgotten. We might experience an unscheduled event in our lives, a health crisis, or a job change. We often find ourselves carrying unnecessary baggage. The Apostle Paul called it "weight:"

> Therefore, since we have so great a cloud of witnesses surrounding us, let us also lay aside every encumbrance and the sin which so easily entangles us, and let us run with endurance the race that is set before us.
> Hebrews 12:1 NASB

Yes, our yoke gets heavy and our burdens cumbersome. Jesus says, "Come to me, all of you who are tired and are carrying heavy loads. I will give you rest" (Matthew 11:28 New International Readers Version).

AS IS

"DON'T BLAME FATE WHEN THINGS go wrong—Trouble doesn't come from nowhere. It's human! Mortals are born and bred for trouble as certainly as sparks fly upward" (Job 5:6-7 MSG).

Oh my! I mused silently as I prepared my flight plan. The auto-pilot couple approach mode is deferred, and the fuel cross-feed valve is wired open. On top of that, the APU (auxiliary power unit) is inoperative. And with a poor weather forecast, they want us to take this airplane to Richmond tonight as is?

"The return flight captain is not going to be happy tomorrow morning," I said aloud to my flight crew. "The weather will be down all day here in Chicago. This airplane could be out of service tomorrow, and the flight could cancel for lack of an operative autopilot. I certainly wouldn't want a captain leaving me in that position.

"Let's not accept the plane as is. Maintenance should at least get the autopilot back on line. We will let them know now so they can plan the maintenance repair. As is, is not acceptable. Perhaps another airplane is available."

Have you ever bought anything as is? Were you ultimately satisfied with your decision? Most of life's encounters are as is situations. Sometimes we have no control over those situations. Lowering our expectations is one sure way to ease our stress level. This is most certainly true in people relationships.

Yet we sometimes present ourselves as is to other people. We should do better because we are better than that and it's a good way to enable our Christian witness. Scripture says, "Do nothing from selfishness or empty conceit, but with humility of mind regard one another as more important than yourselves" (Philippians 2:3 NASB).

God accepts us as is. He has a love relationship with us. His love compels us to submit to his transforming work in our lives. His acceptance of us as is, is our only hope. We are "as is people" dependent upon his mercy. What a great way to live in relationship with God and his authority. If we live in the lordship of Christ, he can do anything with anything—even us.

THE STANDARD IS ONE HUNDRED PERCENT

Praise the Lord! O give thanks to our Captain for He is good. His flying skills endure forever.
Psalm 106:1 (my paraphrase)

THAT IS NOT QUITE THE way the scripture goes, but speaking of high standards, God is the pilot of the universe and "his ways are perfect." His flying skills last forever.

Did you know that every year the airline pilot's license expires? And he or she must demonstrate his flying skills again to the FAA (Federal Aviation Administration) and also the company. This is the dreaded PC (proficiency check), and the passing grade is 100 percent. Also required is a first-class medical every six months. The FAA is not forgiving.

Once a year after exhaustive self-study and a comprehensive written and oral test, the pilot must earn the right to a four-hour simulator flight test. He must demonstrate his ability to fly and think his way through every conceivable system emergency that one could ever encounter in real-line flying because the airplane is not forgiving. It is not enough just to fly the simulator, but you must stay on exact headings and altitudes at all times.

One of the most exacting maneuvers is an ILS approach (Instrument Landing System). This required procedure takes you down to eighty feet above the runway in poor weather conditions, at 150 miles per hour. You land if you see the runway environment. An eventual landing is required. When you demonstrate this maneuver, then you must demonstrate the same maneuver with an inoperative engine. The simulator is not forgiving either. This flying exam must be by the book, never improvised or modified to your liking.

It is discipline and exactness that keeps the flying public confident and safe in all weather and airplane conditions. The study of manuals, systems procedures, publications, and memory items are never ending. The standard is one hundred percent. The check captain is not forgiving, but this is the only way the airline pilot can return to line flying.

> *Christ not only hears us, but also speaks on our behalf and forgives our shortcomings, even our sins.*

What if our discipleship standard to Christ was 100 percent? Would we ever make it out to the line? Our captain, Christ the Lord, is loving and most forgiving. He wants to lead us to true discipleship. "In the same way, the Holy Spirit helps us when we are weak. We do not know how we should pray, but the Spirit himself prays for us. He prays with groans too deep for words" (Romans 8:26 NIV).

We serve a God who not only hears but also speaks on our behalf and forgives our shortcomings, even our sins. He is not our co-pilot, as some bumper stickers say! He is our perfect captain. We are his first officer. If God is your co-pilot, then you need to swap seats.

OUR RIGHTEOUSNESS

DID YOU KNOW THAT AS you enter an airliner and take your seat there are dozens of concurrent preparations and provisions being accomplished on your behalf assuring the airworthiness of that airplane on which you are about to entrust your life?

There is a team of mechanics conducting visual checks on systems, hidden panels, and fluid levels. Fuel required for your flight is computed and confirmed by the flight crew, according to temperature, density, and weight. A complete log history of all the plane's systems and a visual walk-around are conducted. With all systems go, the aircraft logbook is brought aboard and attested and signed by the captain. Only then can the passenger door be closed. It is all procedural.

The flight crew then reads the final pre-flight checklist. The captain can now declare the airplane airworthy, and you will know it when you feel the release of the parking brake. The airplane is declared legal to fly through the heavens.

How are we "declared righteous?" Is it by taking our seat regularly in church? Is it by reciting a creed, praying a prayer, or participating in a ritual? Is it by a good feeling in worship or trusting the crew up front or signing a logbook of registry? Is it by buying your ticket, paying your tithe, or being baptized? Is it by social contact with fellow Christians, attending Sunday school, and enjoying potluck dinners? Is it by confessing your sins and declaring that you will do better? No! Only God can declare our righteousness. Only he can make us airworthy. He imputes and ascribes his righteousness to us.

The airplane logbook contains every fault and failure of that airplane. Every fault and failure is redeemed and attested within limitations, and the captain ascribes that the logbook is clean. He signs the logbook, thereby declaring the plane airworthy.

God takes the logbook of our lives and cleans it up.

Likewise, our loving God knows our limitations. He takes the logbook of our life and cleans it up—attesting, imputing, ascribing, and declaring our righteousness.

> Because of Abraham's faith, God declared him to be righteous. Now this wonderful truth—that God declared him to be righteous—wasn't just for Abraham's benefit. It was for us too, assuring us that God will also declare us to be righteous if we believe in God, who brought Jesus our Lord back from the dead. He was handed over to die because of our sins, and he was raised from the dead to make us right with God.
> Romans 4:22-25 TLB

> Therefore since we have been made right in God's sight by faith, we have peace with God because of what Jesus Christ our Lord has done for us. Because of our faith, Christ has brought us into this place of highest privilege where we now stand, and we confidently and joyfully look forward to sharing God's glory.
> Romans 5:1-2 TLB

There is absolutely nothing we can do to make ourselves legal or airworthy to fly through the heavens. We must trust the logbook of our lives to his care. "Not by our works, lest any man should boast" (Ephesians 2:9 KJV).

THE UNKNOWN QUADRANT

"THE WEATHER IS LOOKING WORSE," I said to my crew as we taxied west from the gate. "I hope we can find one good way to get out of here."

"Taxi into position and hold," said the tower in my earphone. I repeated the words back and added, "We would like to do a 360-degree turn in position to take a look at the weather radar in all quadrants."

"Roger, let me know when you are ready to go."

I manipulated the radar tilt control as we made the circular turn, and the radar picture confirmed what I saw ahead and left of the departure path. As the skies darkened, there was a way out to clearer skies. We could see a narrow passage of light and escape a longer delay from the weather that was moving in on Cedar Rapids. We would take this window of opportunity and depart.

"Everybody ready?" I asked my flight crew. "Takeoff check."

"Tower, United 332, we're ready for takeoff. Wind check, please."

"Winds one-two-zero, one eight, gusts two-five. Fly runway heading, cleared for takeoff."

"Okay, guys, we're cleared to go."

As I pushed the throttles up and released the brakes, I reminded us to watch for any signs of wind shear and airspeed deviations. The plane leaped forward as I held slight down pressure on the centerline. V-one, V-r, V-two... We broke ground in twenty-eight seconds and began an immediate turn toward the weather opening.

"Tower, we need a heading of 050-degrees for about eight miles."

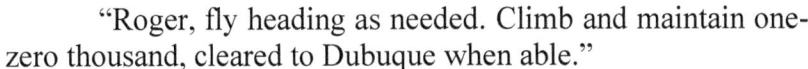

"Roger, fly heading as needed. Climb and maintain one-zero thousand, cleared to Dubuque when able."

"Roger, one-zero thousand, Dubuque when able, United 332."

That day we experienced moderate bumps and heavy rain on climb out but soon cleared the encroaching weather and saved our flying schedule for the day. Our departure had looked doubtful on taxi-out, but the radar showed a path and we were safely underway on time. As we climbed to the east, departure control reported a tornado three miles southwest of the airport. I was glad we were up here rather than down there. We were climbing for blue skies and clear of the encroaching weather.
Insert pix 5 Tornado

My first officer said, "That radar is worth its money, eh?"

"Yes, if it is operated properly," I replied. "But let's not forget, there are times that we can go, but there are also times we must wait."

*We face uncertainty in
unknown quadrants.*

In life, we face uncertainty in unknown quadrants. Sometimes we are headed for trouble and are not even aware of it. We are blindsided and hit turbulence. Our radar is useless in the standby mode, and we cannot see our way through the storms. However, God is faithful when we trust him. He provides a way out because he is the way. "We are hard pressed on every side, but not crushed; perplexed, but not in despair; persecuted, but not abandoned; struck down, but not destroyed" (2 Corinthians 4:8-9 NIV). Proper interpretation and reliance on the radar of his Word enables our faith. We can depart dark skies with God's promises and fly with confidence.

To God be praise!

THE FLIGHT RECORDER

NEVER FLY WITH A PILOT who thinks he is perfect or thinks she never makes a mistake. The flight recorder and its associated cockpit voice recorder prove that pilots are not perfect. These devices record every word and deed by the flight crew. A perfect pilot does not exist. However, only the last thirty minutes of flight remain on the continuous tape. Previous actions are erased and forgotten. (That is good!)

Mental mistakes by pilots are generally caught and accounted for quickly by the crew. In fact, sometimes one pilot may observe his mistake and silently correct it while chiding and confessing to himself. (Experience is a great teacher.) However, if mistakes lead to what we call "an event," then, "Houston, we have a problem," and a blip is made on the flight recorder tape.

The flight crew does not cause all the problems. Aircraft systems all interrelate to each other. For example, mechanically:

- an engine fails in flight
- the landing gear will not go up or come down
- the cabin pressurization or electrical system fails
- or maybe the plane hits severe clear air turbulence

Pilots are trained to handle these events, but the blip is still on the tape. The flight crew must take care of these problems, but how they solve the problem is judged as well. Exactness and knowledge is what piloting is all about.

Words, thoughts, and deeds in our lives may seem insignificant but can lead to an event that might become a blip on the tape. We all interrelate to each other. Quickly repent, ask for forgiveness, confess it to God and do not let it become a blip (or a sin) on your flight recorder tape. Remember, like the flight recorder, your previous sins can be erased, forgiven, and forgotten. "Let the words of my mouth and the meditation of my heart be acceptable in Thy sight, O Lord, my Strength and my Redeemer" (Psalm 19:14 KJV).

Keep the blips off your flight recorder and have a good flight today.

WEIGHT AND BALANCE

AIRLINE PASSENGERS RARELY GIVE A thought to the weight and balance of a flight. However, flight regulations require the pilot to perform a weight and balance calculation before every takeoff. Not only must the airplane be at or under maximum allowable takeoff weight at that particular temperature and altitude, but the load must also be balanced evenly, not nose heavy or tail heavy. Even potential turbulence can be a factor. If pilots operate outside these parameters, they place themselves into a "test pilot" regime. They are flirting with disaster on takeoff or landing.

I have seen instances when it was necessary to delay flight waiting for cooler temperatures before taking off from Sky Harbor Airport in Phoenix (118 degrees F is not on the takeoff chart). It is not unusual during the hot summer at Denver International Airport to burn off unused taxi fuel before taking the runway.

Is it time to sit down and do a weight and balance calculation in your life?

What kind of load are you carrying? What are your operating parameters? Are you "maxed out?" Is your life unbalanced? Is the heat too high, the air too thin? Are you flying through turbulent skies? Have you calculated the risk? Is it time to sit down and do a weight and balance calculation in your life?

It is so easy to get maxed out—financially, mentally, and physically. We are tempted to carry too much load in turbulent and poor conditions when we might need to wait a while. There is a song that says, "What a difference a day makes; twenty-four little hours."

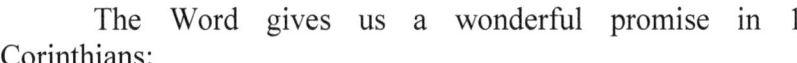

The Word gives us a wonderful promise in 1 Corinthians:

> No temptation has overtaken you but such as is common to man; and God is faithful, who will not allow you to be tempted beyond what you are able, but with the temptation will provide the way of escape also, so that you will be able to endure it. (Corinthians 10:13 NASB)

However, with this promise comes a warning, verse 12: "Therefore let him who thinks he stands take heed lest he fall."

WHEN THINGS GET BENT

THE TELEPHONE RANG, SUDDENLY JOLTING me awake. It was 5:30 a.m. I was the only one in our apartment pad that morning at the crash pad hotel that leased rooms to airline pilots on reserve. I knew it was the crew desk with a flight assignment. I turned on the lamp, reached for the telephone, and trying to sound awake said, "Hello, Captain Brumbeloe speaking."

"Morning, Captain Brumbeloe; we have a non-revenue flight for you this morning. The purpose of the flight is to fill out a documentation form of how the airplane flies at various speeds, altitudes, trim settings, and flap configurations. We also need autopilot certification for this airplane coming out of maintenance. You'll meet your flight crew at flight ops, and we'll bus you over to the maintenance hangar at 8:30. You can get the details of the assignment there. Any questions?"

I thought to myself, *Oh, brother, this must be a bent airplane. It's got rigging problems or maybe an inspection for a hard landing.*

No passengers, no flight attendants, no coffee! Boring holes in the sky for three hours with no particular place to go, just documenting how the airplane flies. No destination but a round robin, O'Hare back to O'Hare in a bent airplane. It was a unique assignment.

Sound boring? Actually, it wasn't! There is much to be learned in an airplane with flight controls that need to be rigged and trim tabs that need to be documented at various flap configurations. You learn a lot about flight-control positioning, spoiler float with and without the autopilot, and roll rates at different airspeeds. Airplanes need to be in proper rig for good control and fuel efficiency in order to get back on the line carrying families to destinations.

*Our lives can get bent out of
shape by sin or a hard landing.*

Things do get bent. Even our Christian lives can get bent out of shape by sin or a hard landing. We too often need retrimming. Our lives need to be in proper rig for good control and efficiency in order to get back on line for our families' sakes.

Consider this great Charles Wesley praise and prayer hymn:

> Breathe, O breathe Thy loving Spirit,
> Into every troubled breast!
> Let us all in Thee inherit;
> Let us find that second rest.
> Take away our bent to sinning;
> Alpha and Omega be;
> End of faith, as its beginning,
> Set our hearts at liberty.
>
> "Love Divine, All Loves Excelling."
> Hymn by Charles Wesley, 1747; verse 2

PART FOUR

THE ADVANCED JOURNEY

"WHAT DOES IT TAKE TO be a captain, anyway?" That's a question first officers mockingly ask their captain when they make an observation or a flight decision that later proves correct.

An experienced captain possesses an advanced skill. It might even be called a sixth sense, one of sensing uncertainty or avoiding situations that could lead away from normal flight operations.

I believe we all can experience this sixth sense in life as we master knowledge, un-clutter our minds and accept responsibility.

I felt this skill developing as a first officer as I took care of my captain, gaining his trust and nods of approval. I knew I was flying well ahead of the airplane, making correct and timely decisions, never having to scurry to catch up.

I had a steady hand and new confidence. I knew I was ready for the captain's seat. I would step up to new preparation to put my signature on the flight papers.

I set the parking brake and with a sigh of relief and satisfaction, contemplated my low visibility, engine out approach, and landing. We had landed safely. I switched to the cabin intercom and commanded the passengers to remain seated. As I stared out the windshield at the runway centerline beneath us, I was hoping that my four-hour check ride was over. The FAA check pilot, sitting in the dark behind me, spoke up.

"Captain Brumbeloe, I welcome you as United Airline's newest captain. Nice job! Congratulations!"

I felt subdued in my moment of ecstasy. My flying career was forever changed. My dream had come true. I was now a captain at a major airline. I would go to work in the left seat.

I remember as a teenager my mother's words. What insight she had. She spoke so clearly: "Life is hard, but you can achieve it! Get a new grip and go. You can do it when you make up your mind to do it."

*The things that must not change
must take priority in our lives.*

We awake every morning to a different world. We face changing times, all the while knowing there are things we cannot change. More importantly, the things that must not change must take priority in our lives. Core values, commitments, and vows hold us steady in difficult and pressured times. We live in an exciting world. Challenging, yes, but there is never a dull moment. We have a wonderful destination. We cannot imagine what joy we will experience when we land. "Eye has not seen nor ear heard, nor has it entered into the heart of man what God has prepared for those who love him" (1 Corinthians 2:9 KJV). Our diligence, perseverance, and sacrifice are not for an earthly goal but a world without end, heavenly prize.

A CERTAIN WORD

"CAPTAIN" JIM, THE SECOND OFFICER, spoke to me with a certain tone. "We've lost oil quantity and pressure on the number-three engine gauges. The EGT is out of parameters."

I scanned the engine gages and confirmed his certain word. I knew we had an emergency on our hands.

"Select bus number one with your essential power selector, and let's shutdown engine number three." I spoke calmly as I recalled the memorized checklist. "Confirm number three throttle going to idle; confirm number three engine fuel lever going to shutoff."

The cockpit yawed slightly right, indicating engine shutdown. I trimmed a twist of left rudder to maintain aircraft heading and adjusted the power. I continued. "Confirm and pull the number-three engine fire shutoff handle. Don't fire the bottle for now. Let's read the engine shutdown checklist."

"Okay, Captain," said Jim as he flipped several switches.

"Bob, you fly the airplane. Let's slow to 250 knots and maintain flight level two-five-zero. I'll call the first flight attendant up to the flight deck and brief her and work with Jim on the rest of the checklists."

I spoke softly into my microphone. "Denver Center, United 700, we are declaring an emergency. We have performed a precautionary shutdown on number-three engine. We have 33,000 pounds of fuel remaining and 156 souls on board. Everything else seems nominal. Could you inform our company, please? Over."

"Roger, United 700. This is Denver Center. Understand you have declared an emergency. We will contact your company. 'Squawk' 7600, say intentions."

"Center, United 700 requesting diversion into Denver International, and we'll take a heading and lower altitude. For precautions, we request the emergency equipment to standby on landing. We can accept an approach clearance in about fifteen minutes. And can you get the Denver weather for us, over?"

"Denver Center, affirmative. Standby."

"Bob, can you talk to ATC while I brief Nancy and the passengers?"

I stifled a brave yawn…and so goes the certain word of CQT (Captain Qualification Training) in the aircraft simulator—necessary, exact language, and good training.

Every flight situation requires a certain word of procedural communication and ability to stay calm and collected in anxious moments of flight. These procedures must be practiced to assure a safe landing.

In real situations of life, we all need to practice a certain word in our lives and our relationships. Calm words like: "I believe in you." "You are a trusted friend." "I appreciate you."
We also need to speak certain words to those we love and influence, words like: "Thank you." "I love you." "You did a great job." "You can depend on me." But more importantly, we must also speak the certain word of our faith in confession, asking for God's help to keep our commitment to him amid our daily struggles. Our spiritual lives may not always have all engines running, but God promises to help us in our troubles.

Young person or seasoned flyer, remember when the going gets rough, our help comes from the Lord. He is at our side. His Word is our checklist and assures us of a safe landing. "The Lord is our refuge and strength, a very present help in time of trouble" (Psalm 46:1 KJV). He is the certain Word, the Word of Life.

THE IMPORTANCE OF TAXIING

TAXIING AND AIRPLANE IS NOT as impressive as flying the airplane, but you cannot fly an airplane straight to the gate. You also cannot takeoff from the gate. We must taxi first. It's not unusual to taxi three to six miles before takeoff using a curculios route. It is time we give taxiing its due. Takeoffs and landings must include a taxi. Takeoffs begin with the taxi, and landings end with the taxi…a lowly taxi.

Do you remember the event of Princess Diana's death? It was in the news for months. She was famous for being famous. Do you remember another death that same week? Mother Teresa. Need I make the point?

The taxi saves the landing!

We always want to talk about the landing or the takeoff…the pilot's glory. Who cares about taxiing? However, improper taxiing can lead to accidents on takeoff, and inability to convert a landing into a taxi can lead to running off the runway. All pilots know that the taxi serves the takeoff and the taxi saves the landing. Jesus said, "If you will be great in the Kingdom, you must become a servant" (Mark 10:43 ESV). Paraphrased, perhaps this means you must know how to taxi. Jesus asked, "Do you covet the right hand of the Father?" In addition, Matthew 20:20 poses this question: "Are you able to drink the cup?" Verse 22 asks, "Will you wash each others' feet?"

We easily see faults in others and we tend to enjoy the spotlight until it reveals our own shortcomings and deficiencies. There is glory in the takeoff and landing, but what about the lowly taxi? Taxiing is the servant to the takeoff, and the savior of the landing. Good takeoffs and landings are the glory, but taxiing gets us to the gate, our final destination. The lowly servant serves best. The life of Mother Teresa is proof.

THE NERVE CENTER OF FAITH

THE FLIGHT DECK IS THE nerve center of aircraft operation, but more importantly it is the nerve center of faith. It is what the pilot believes to be true. The flight deck is where his faith is reconciled and all things hold together.

No pilot would strap himself into an airplane for flight if he did not believe that airplane would fly. Before he boards the plane, he reads the maintenance history of the airplane, a summary of every mechanical action taken in this marvelous machine of flight. This document is his basis for belief, the all-in-all of documents.

Before he begins his flight planning for this flight, he is skeptical. Now, he is a believer, and his fears have been dispelled. He knows the airplane is good and airworthy. He trusts his most precious cargo to fly on that plane. He believes in every switch, every system, and the laws of physics that will propel this airplane into the heavens. The flight deck is the nerve center of his faith and confidence.

We must not take the nerve center of our Christian faith so complacently. We have to
believe by faith, but we cannot take the Bible at face value lying on the coffee table. "For I am confident of this very thing, that He who began a good work in you will perfect it until the day of Christ Jesus" (Philippians 1:6 NASB). The fact that we must believe by faith makes it doubly important to know what we believe by faith, and whom we trust.

This great scripture describes Jesus, the nerve center of our Christian faith:

> He is the image of the invisible God, the firstborn of all creation. For by him all things were created, in heaven and on earth, visible and invisible, whether thrones or dominions or rulers or authorities—all things were created through him and for him. And he is before all things, and in

him all things hold together. And he is the head of the body, the church. He is the beginning, the firstborn from the dead, that in everything he might be preeminent. For in him all the fullness of God was pleased to dwell, and through him to reconcile to himself all things, whether on earth or in heaven, making peace by the blood of his cross.
Colossians 1:15-20 (HCSB)

Prayer: Dear Lord, your Word is the nerve center of our faith. You come to us as the God of relationships. It is in you that all things hold together. Thank you for your empirical and trustworthy Word. Teach us anew the evidence of our faith, which is your love for us. Your love dispels our fears. Help us to submit our lives to you in love and service. We pray in your name, Jesus. Amen.

KNOWLEDGE DEDICATED TO A SMALLER FRAMEWORK

WHAT I AM ABOUT TO relate to you is a bit difficult for me. Over a period of time, I realized that developing a personal culture of flight safety was learning not to push the parameters of flight even though it fell within legal limitations.

This event happened almost two decades ago when I was a first officer, but as I have relived some of my flying memories, the question still haunts me. We have all experienced that confession is good for the soul. So here it goes.

We were flying into National Airport DC (now Reagan International), and the landing winds were at max demonstrated crosswinds limit. I had a sense of uncertainty. The visibility was good, but lurking danger could be ahead of us.

The Captain had asked me if I was comfortable to execute the landing. I knew that a strong left crosswind landing executed from the right seat (first officer seat) provided better visibility of the runway from the flight deck because of bank and crab angles required in those flight conditions.

I told him, "Yes, sir, no offense to you, but I'd rather do the landing than watch the landing."

I think he was relieved.

We told the passengers that we might have to divert to Baltimore because of high winds as we watched an American flight execute a go-around in front of us. With the winds from 270 degrees at thirty-five knots with some gusts to forty-two, I suggested we change to runway 33, the short runway.

I re-briefed the approach and landing and made it very clear that I had no expectation of touching down but just to shoot the approach to take a look. I knew at the last second we might continue and land. (In reality this is called flirting with temptation because that's what pilots do…we land!) Pilots defend this thinking because all landings have the mentality of a go-around even in normal conditions.

All the way down final approach, we were buffeted by the swirling winds. Eighty feet above the runway, I added power, kicked right rudder to align the 727 nose with the runway, and announced, "I'm at right rudder limits." It was momentary, so I continued the approach. We were lined up on the runway centerline at near maximum left bank. Fifty, thirty, ten sang out the radar altimeter; we touched down. It was hard work, but it worked out well.

I released backpressure on the controls, deployed the ground spoilers, went into reverse thrust while applying full ailerons into the wind, and braked to a motivated stop while fighting to stay on the centerline with the rudder pedals. We had made a max performance landing on runway 33 using only 3,500 feet.

It only took a few seconds after touchdown.

"You've got the airplane, Captain," I said.

Then I realized I was breathing heavy. Flying does not have to be that much work.

I could hear the passengers cheering in the cabin. They were glad we did not divert. I was proud, but at the same time, I felt ashamed as I heard their response. Perhaps I had landed

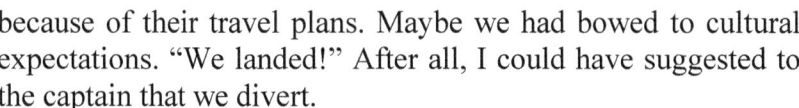

because of their travel plans. Maybe we had bowed to cultural expectations. "We landed!" After all, I could have suggested to the captain that we divert.

The haunting question remains, "Did we distort safety that day?" We definitely dedicated our knowledge to a smaller framework. I later told this story to an experienced captain that I did not know very well. He was not impressed! He jumped on it.

"What a (expletive) foolish thing to do. You did not have to do that! You could have bent an airplane." Then he added, "As you gain experience you will get more restrictive, not more liberal. That's what keeps us all safe."

"You didn't have to do that," kept ringing in my head. In other words, what he meant was: safety is the ultimate motivation! Safety rises above all other motivations. Safety cannot be relegated to a smaller framework.

Although my captain had trusted me to shoot the approach into National Airport and we were able to land, I have been haunted reliving our decisions that day and their implications. I am convinced that we made the wrong decision, flirting with crosswind limits and operating with the wrong motivation. I was too agreeable and have not flown that close to crosswind limits since then.

As we gain experience, our standards will get tighter, not more liberal.

Why have I related this story? I have recently read Wilbur Wilberforce's book *Real Christianity*. Although written more than two hundred years ago, he unpacks the way we tend to live the Christian life in the framework of our culture. Wilberforce says for the Christian, "The Holy Spirit is our ultimate motivation." In other words, the Holy Spirit rises above all other motivations. The Holy Spirit cannot be relegated to a smaller framework in our lives. Our lives must not be lived in sacred and secular frameworks. As we gain experience in the Christian life, our standards will get tighter, not more liberal. We just don't have to do some things. Indeed, we cease doing things because of our advancement.

Here are Wilberforce's thoughts from page 70 of his book:

> We wrongly assume "If I meet my religious obligations, [as in a legal crosswind limitation] I am free to live my life as I wish." Thus, the reality and work of the Holy Spirit are held captive in a diminished role in our lives. Authentic faith is not allowed to expand and possess more of our lives. Wow! When Christ is not free to possess more and more of who we are, the tendency over time is to take even what we have placed within the smaller framework and move it out into the larger context. We will actually regress spiritually instead of progressing in true spirituality. The space occupied by faith will diminish over time, until it is hardly active at all.
>
> *Real Christianity*; William Wilberforce, 1797; Revised and Updated by Bob Beltz; Regal Books, Gospel Light; Ventura, California, U.S.A.

This is the genesis of cultural Christianity. In reality, it is a degenerative process. Wilberforce speaks to principles critical to living an authentic Christian life:

- He passionately describes how the essential beliefs of Christianity have been distorted (for example, it's okay to try to land)

- He clearly shows how concepts of sin, evil, and depravity have been watered down (limitations can't be that important)

- He challenges Christians to maintain a biblical lifestyle (fly by the Spirit of the Book)

Prayer: Dear Lord, dear merciful Lord, forgive us. Help us. Let us not bow to the cultural crosswinds that buffet our lives. Help us to live fully in the ultimate motivation of your Holy Spirit. Amen.

AMBIGUITY ON THE FLIGHT DECK

WE WILL FACE AMBIGUITY IN our lives. That is a fact. During these times, spiritual protocol helps us find our way.

The word *ambiguity* means "doubtfulness" or "uncertainty of meaning or intention." It also means an "unclear, indefinite, or equivocal word or course of action in the face of conflicting information." Ambiguity on the flight deck results because of the loss of situational awareness, and once detected, it is a very uncomfortable thing to well-trained pilots. The natural human response is to try to ignore it, but airline training programs clearly teach all pilots to confront it quickly and make a book-based decision. It is important for someone to speak up and say, "Hey, let's talk about this."

Sometimes, ambiguity shows up as conflicting aircraft system indications, aircraft performance, navigation, or instrument errors. However, the most subtle ambiguities in the cockpit come from induced human sources requiring interpretation. For example:

- An unclear ATC clearance
- Flying in dynamic weather conditions
- Interpreting the weather radar
- Intentions of a fellow crewmember in flight decisions

Good communications on the flight deck are imperative in solving ambiguity. Fortunately, one statement I have never heard in the cockpit is "I told you so." We must lay aside personal differences and disagreements and fly by the book. We can talk about differences after we safely land. Pilots are quick to forget and move beyond mistakes. No one likes to hear, "I told you so," even though it seems to bring pleasure to utter those words. It's much better to say, "Hey, let's talk about this before we get ourselves into a predicament." Solving ambiguity before takeoff is always the better course of action.

> *Often we accept ambiguities in our lives with little concern until a major problem arises and catches us unaware.*

Back on the ground, how often we accept ambiguities in our lives with little concern until a major problem arises and catches us unaware. Our immediate response is to pass the blame or take inappropriate action making matters worse. It is not possible to be ambiguous about God's laws without consequences. However, we often choose to ignore ambiguity and live our lives making no clear choices until the choice is taken away.

Ladies and gentlemen, we have arrived at that gate. We must pay attention now. The age of information has become the age of ambiguity. Political correctness has changed the meaning of words and truth is blurred. However, there are no moral second considerations with God. Politicians often speak ambiguously—uncertain, unclear, with indefinite words. They equivocate. Nevertheless, followers of Christ are without excuse but full of hope. God speaks clearly. His Word is specific. His Word is truth, no ambiguity. God's Word speaks clearly on the flight deck of our lives. His justice and righteousness will reign. We can live with hope and certainty.

We will talk about it endlessly…after we land.

BRUSH WITH 9/11

THE INFAMOUS DAY OF 9/11 changed the landscape of the world in one event. It did so by using US airliners as bombs to crash into the World Trade Center twin towers in New York City and the Pentagon in Washington DC. Another plane was thwarted from the White House and crashed in Pennsylvania.

I completed my week of flying the day before 9/11 and caught a flight home that evening. I was on days off the next morning as millions of us watched our televisions in disbelief when a second plane crashed in the second tower of the World Trade Center. I knew immediately, without question, that the planes had been commandeered by terrorists and that the US aviation system would have to shut down immediately for an extended time. We were under attack of an unknown magnitude.

The next morning I was shocked when I saw the names and pictures of all nineteen suicide hijackers on the front page of our newspaper. One name and picture was all too familiar—Hani Hanjour, a mustached, thin-faced, so-called Arabian Airlines pilot. He had (legally) jump-seated my airplane the morning of September 1 on a flight out of Detroit. I recognized his picture in the newspaper and went to my flight bag and retrieved the jump-seat stub printout that authorized his jump-seat privilege. His name matched the jump-seat stub.

I immediately called my chief pilot and related the details of that September 1st morning and the flight to Denver. The following day I called the FBI and for two hours voluntarily answered questions about that early morning flight from Detroit. I related to them that my close encounter with 9/11 had occurred ten days earlier, on September 1st on a 6:30 morning flight from Detroit to Denver.

Although the FBI volunteered no information to me, I deduced from their leading questions that they already knew most of the information. As we now know, a fifth airplane was reported planned to be flown into the Sears tower as it passed Chicago.

Before I relate this story I hasten to tell you that airline flight crews since the early days of hijacking had been trained to watch and report suspicious activities and security breaches. It included any break from protocol, securing airport door codes, property and equipment, identification tags, uniforms, flight bags, and transportation to and from the airport to layover hotels.

This was before the US government created the TSA (transportation security authority). Although screening and metal detectors had been ramped up in all US airports, passenger screening was still by contract with airport and airline authorities.

Here are the details of the event.

We (my flight crew and flight attendants) arrived at the Detroit Metro Airport that September 1 morning at 5:30 to proceed through an almost empty screening checkpoint. There were five screeners manning the security gate; three of them wore turban headdresses.

As I approached the metal detector, I was instructed to remove my uniform coat and captain's hat. I refused to remove my coat (I would not disrobe), but I did surrender my hat for inspection. Then my flight bag was held and I was informed that it would be opened and inspected. Unless I could watch the removal and replacement of all the items in my bag, they would not open it, I asserted. This offending screening agent was obviously the oldest of the agents on duty and wore a turban. I looked at another turban-dressed agent and asked, "What's going on here? This kind of check is highly inappropriate and unnecessary."

The agent simply smiled, winked at me, and whispered, "He's old." The rest of my crew had already gone through and were watching the proceedings.

After I retrieved my hat, suitcase, and flight bag I rejoined my crew and we walked toward flight operations. It was then that I remarked to them, "Do you feel safe now with the concert of frivolity that I just experienced at the screening station? I mean, men in turbans making a spectacle of checking a flight crew?

I dismissed the idea as cosmetic measures of security for public consumption and turned my thoughts to flight planning our flight to Denver. I left flight operations at 6:05 for the airplane, briefed the flight attendants, and "made my nest" in the captain seat.

Our crew quickly settled in, and we performed our pre-departure checks and read the checklists. We had a northwest pilot from Detroit on one of our jump seats and we all chatted about the airline industry news. We treat our qualified pilot "brothers" as a welcome guest, knowing they understand the jump seat rules and protocol.

At 6:29 a second "jump seater" presented himself, and I heard the front cabin door slam shut. Our second officer said, "Captain, we have another jump seater."

I looked back and said, "Sorry. I can't let you ride. You should have been here fifteen minutes ago. It's departure time, and I don't have the time for your bags or briefing. You'll have to deplane."

The second officer said, "Captain, they've already closed the front door, and he only has a knapsack bag."

I replied, "Sorry. I cannot accommodate him. He should know the protocol. Get the gate agent back and tell her to open the door." I sensed a tension in the cockpit, but I did not care about being politically correct or even accommodating. Jump seat protocol was a part of my operational rules.

The tug driver called from below and said, "Captain, you are cleared to release your brakes."

I said "Standby. We need the gate agent back."

The second officer called our flight operations and requested the jet bridge and door to be opened. We got no response. We waited. I then called our load planner and requested the jet bridge and gate agent. The load planner said, "Captain, we are short handed here, and she has already left the gate to service another flight."

"Thanks," I replied.

I looked at the jump seater, took his printout stub, and noticed his name and airline, which read Hani Hanjour, "Saudi Arabian Airlines." I had seen a couple of these before. I consulted my "do not ride list" and told the jump seater to have a seat. I would suspend my rules and not delay the flight any longer.

We performed the before-push checklist and then called the tug driver. "Hello, below! Brakes released, you are cleared to push."

As we climbed through 28,000 feet, we passed Chicago and could plainly see the Sears Tower and downtown area nestled up against Lake Michigan. We remarked that it was a nice scene.

Leveling at 35,000, I looked back to ask Hani if he had flown the night before. He suddenly leaned back as if he were sleeping. I attempted no further conversation at that time.

I did not like the proceedings, but he was legal in the computer. I decided this fellow simply did not speak English well and did not know the jump seat protocol. That would be confirmed later in the flight when Hani left the flight deck to go to the lavatory without checking with me. When I looked back and Hani was not there, I asked the second officer, "Where's Hani?"

The second officer said, "He asked to go to the lavatory."

"Again, that's not protocol," I said.

The second officer apologized and said, "Captain, that's my mistake. From now on I will make sure it is with the captain's permission."

"Does he know the (secret) knock? Go back and check it out. Make sure he's alone, and you escort him back."

I actually did not suspect anything at all, except that we had not followed our cockpit jump seat rules protocol closely enough, and vowed never to let anyone who could not speak good English ride my jump seat again.

When we arrived in Denver at the gate, without warning, Hani jumped out and was gone without a word. Again, no protocol. I told my crew I would never allow another Saudi

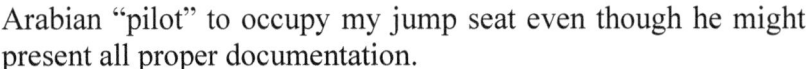

Arabian "pilot" to occupy my jump seat even though he might present all proper documentation.

In retrospect, the airlines had a system in place for confirming jump seat privileges. We had a "no fly list" that was updated every week, and the captain had the right to refuse honoring anyone the privilege. However, that system had been circumvented and corrupted, as we learned on 9/11.

Political correctness had blurred the truth and failed the system...

You can imagine my angry consternation that morning when I recognized the jump-seater's picture in the paper.

The 9/11 Commission made it seem as if airline crews had never heard of Mohammed Atta. Not true! He was a known terrorist, and his name topped our "do not ride list of imposters" who had posed themselves as approved pilot crewmembers. Pilot training had been adequate, but the system was flawed and had far too many weak links. Political correctness had blurred the truth and failed the system...all the more reason to operate on rules of protocol.

The very reason for political correctness is to blur the truth. It was true in the biblical history of Rome, Jerusalem, and Athens...in the advent of the coming of the promised Messiah. Jesus himself refused to bow to the Pharisees when he called them vipers and hypocrites...but advised them to render to Caesar what is Caesar's and to God what is God's.

Wisdom does not allow political correctness to blur the truth. Wisdom comes from following God's laws, not man's rules. When reason overtakes revelation, we are goners.

"O Lord, I know that the way of man is not in himself: it is not in man that walks to direct his steps" (Jeremiah 10:23 American King James Version).

"A man's heart plans his way, but the Lord directs his steps" (Proverbs 16:9 NKJV).

"Thorns and snares are in the way of the perverse; He who guards himself will be far from them" (Proverbs 22:5 NASB).

AMBIGUITY UNCHECKED

WOULD YOU AGREE WITH ME that you would never get on an airplane if you thought the flight crew was ambiguous to the flight? Ambiguity simply cannot be tolerated on the flight deck. The famous Northwest Airline flight 188 that over flew Minneapolis on October 21, 2009, is such an example. You might recall that this flight crew was out of contact with ATC for about an hour.

If I may give an extreme example: It is like saying it does not matter where or when a plane lands. Just take off, fly a while, select an airport, and land. No! We would not tolerate such an ambiguous attitude from the pilot crew. Yet we live our lives in an ambiguous age. Perhaps our tolerance has gone mad. When ambiguity turns into ambivalence, nothing matters. An airline captain cannot afford to be ambivalent.

I once had an aloof flight attendant on a flight delayed at the gate. She came to the flight deck and sat down where she proceeded to do her nails. I had already informed the passengers that we had a mechanical delay for a yet undetermined amount of time and would keep them advised as to the nature of the delay.

I looked back and saw a first-class passenger (a frequent flyer) go into the flight attendant's galley and proceed to look for a cup of coffee. There was none brewing. I suggested to the flight attendant that since our flight was delayed she might attend to the first-class passengers' needs. She never looked up but replied that she had decided not to serve drinks until after takeoff. It raised my eyebrows a bit. I got out of my seat and went to the galley to assist the passenger.

He said, "Captain, I see that you have more than a mechanical problem here."

I thanked him for his patience and told him I would take care of it.

I suspected there had been some relational problems. I proceeded to the rear of the aircraft to confer with the other flight attendants and discovered that there had been a big unresolved conflict on an earlier flight. By this time, everyone in the first-class section knew what was going on. I took my time and returned to the flight deck. The flight attendant was still doing her nails.

I approached her and said, "Madam, we need to talk. I am not going to address the differences with your crew that you brought on board today. However, I cannot accept your ambivalence to your fellow crew members and to our passengers. I need you on the team back there."

She responded, "Captain, I don't need you to tell me how to do my job."

That was enough discussion for me. I stepped out to the phone on the jet bridge, called zone operations, and requested a replacement flight attendant. I explained that I could not trust my passenger's safety to her ambivalent attitude or to my captain's authority should we experience a problem in flight. I returned to the flight deck and suggested that the flight attendant take a reassignment. She was off the flight. It was not a pleasant experience and one I would never experience again.

There is simply no place on the flight deck of our lives for ambivalence to take root. And it is dangerous to compromise right principles for any desired unity. We all experience ambiguity. However, we must not let the ambiguity of this age turn into ambivalence in our lives. We all have family and friends who are depending on us. Truth matters. We do not proceed to our destination by default.

> *Ambivalence is a step beyond ambiguity,*
> *one of yielding to temptation, and*
> *is worse than being lukewarm.*

Ambiguity and temptation in itself are not a sin. But ambivalence is a step beyond ambiguity, one of yielding to temptation, and is worse than being lukewarm. We all remember that Jesus did not like the taste of lukewarm. A divided heart leads to lukewarm ambiguity. The Holy Scripture reminds us, "Then, when desire has conceived, it gives birth to sin; and sin, when it is full-grown, brings forth death" (James 1:15 NIV). In other words, ambivalence, when it has conceived, turns into "nothing matters," and "nothing matters" brings the death of truth and relationships in our lives.

It does matter where we land…where we come down on matters of truth. Don't let the desire for unity compromise flight operations.

FAITH IN ACTION

CHRISTIAN FAITH HAS A WAY of seeing the whole picture even when the whole picture is not available. While still at the gate, an airline pilot knows there are storms out there even though he cannot see them. However, he also knows that after takeoff, the plane's radar will display these storms and he can trust it to guide him throughout his journey. He puts his faith into action.

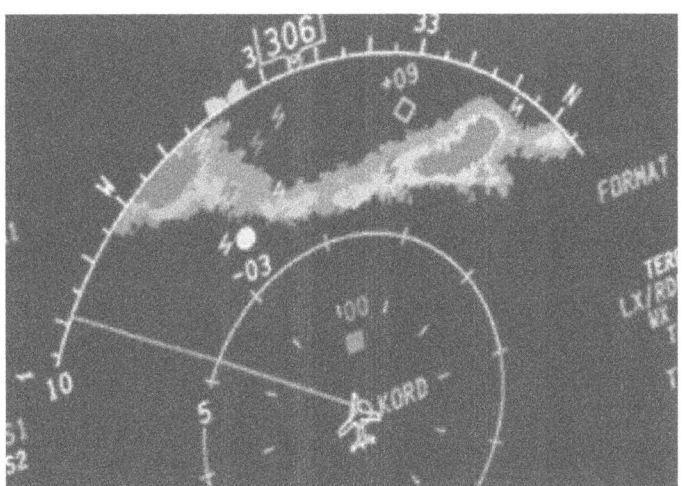

Let us suppose that a certified captain refuses to take off until all storms have dissipated. In essence, he is refusing to put into action that which the airplane was designed to do. He demonstrates a lack of faith in action. Mechanics can do all the checklists, start the engines, and taxi the airplane. For example, often at Chicago O'Hare, ground control will say, "Give way to the 737; he's going to the hangar." Mechanics taxi to the hangar.

They obviously know the airplane very well, but they cannot put into action that for which the airplane is designed to accomplish.

Do you ever feel like a mechanic with your faith? You can start the engines and perhaps even taxi to the hangar, but you never turn the airplane into the wind and take off. Just taxiing around with your faith is pretty well useless.

Recall the story in Mark 2:3: Four men came bringing their paralyzed friend on a mat to Jesus. Skeptics wanting to debate Jesus filled the house. Unable to shove their way in, yet believing so strongly that Jesus would heal their friend, they cut a hole in the roof and lowered him straight down in front of the skeptics in the room. Now that was faith in action!

Faith, without action, makes us recipients of what our culture shoves at us.

Our faith is always in danger of being restricted by a secular worldview creeping into the church. Many dangerous ideas and misleading promises exist in a secular worldview of faith. A passive faith, or faith without action, makes us recipients of what our culture shoves at us. Faith is not merely wishful thinking about a determined future; faith is about an action of that which we already possess and what God has promised. A confession of faith does not stand alone but must be proved. Faith is taking a risk. Faith must be put into action.

Hear these words so poignantly written by Bill and Gloria Gaither:

> Help me take the risk of losing,
>
> Lose it all to find in choosing
>
> To believe you are the answer;
>
> Earth and heaven reconciled.
>
> "I Do Believe"; Words and Music by Bill and Gloria Gaither, Gaither Music Company

Like the four men on the roof, our faith in action brings earth and heaven together. It is worth cutting a hole in the roof!

SPIRITUAL MAINTENANCE

"TEACH ME YOUR WAY, O Lord; I will walk in your truth; Unite my heart to fear your name" (Psalm 86:1 NASB).

As recently as 2009, some major airlines had failed to comply with timely airworthiness directives known as ADs. As a result, hundreds of airline flights were canceled because they failed to meet the FAA required checks on schedule.

ADs are issued from the Federal Aviation Administration when regular aircraft maintenance reveals problems with parts and procedures. The FAA shares this information with all airlines, and all must comply within the grace period. Without compliance, the airplane's airworthiness certificate is suspended.

These airworthiness directives included:

- Frayed wiring bundles that connect aircraft systems
- Rudder yaw damper systems and suspect valves
- Sub-standard landing gear parts and cargo bay fire warning sensors

There was nothing apparently wrong with these planes, but lurking danger existed until maintenance ADs could be accomplished.

Is flying safe in the United States? Yes, absolutely, as long as airlines never consider maintenance lightly. There is no such thing as "light maintenance," and there are no shortcuts. There is but one authority. An aircraft mechanic cannot interpret what seems right or convenient when performing maintenance.

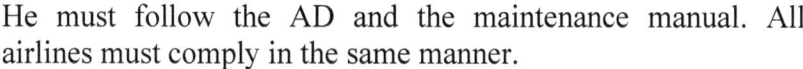

He must follow the AD and the maintenance manual. All airlines must comply in the same manner.

The Holy Spirit gently reminds us that there are no shortcuts in becoming his disciple.

We seem to like shortcuts. We often try to employ them in various areas of our lives. Nevertheless, regular spiritual maintenance in our lives often reveals shortcomings and lurking dangers. God gives us spiritual directives in the Bible. Sometimes we fail to comply with them, but his Holy Spirit gently reminds us that there are no shortcuts in becoming his disciple. We must follow the spiritual ADs in his Word. Despite the eclectic voices in religious circles, God's directives are trustworthy. There is but one authority. God has shared his directives with all of us. Today, in our postmodern mood, where truth, meaning, and certainty are a matter of interpretation, "lite" is not God's directive.

> Jesus said to them all, "If anyone would come after me, he must deny himself and take up his cross daily and follow me. For whoever wants to save his life will lose it, but whoever loses his life for me will save it." Luke 9:23-24 NIV

C.S. Lewis sums up the difficult application of this verse for all of us in this when he writes:

> The terrible thing, the almost impossible thing, is to hand over your whole self—all your wishes and precautions—to Christ.
> Christ says, "Give me All. I do not want so much of your time and so much of your money and so much of your work: I want you. I have not come to torment your natural self, but to kill it. No half measures are any good. I don't want to cut off a branch here and a branch there, I want to have the whole tree down."
> C.S. Lewis, Counting the Cost; *Mere Christianity*; Harper Collins, Publisher

THE NARROW GATE

"ENTER YE IN AT THE straight gate for wide is the gate and broad is the way that leads to destruction and many there be which go in thereof. Because straight is the gate and narrow is the way which leads unto life and few there be that find it" (Matthew 7:13-14 KJV).

My friend Dave Dedman is an air traffic controller specialist in one of the busiest approach sectors in the USA. He recently reminded me of the narrow gate mentioned in Matthew 7 and that distraction is the greatest enemy of the church.

Dave controls the Bowie approach transition just fifty miles northwest of DFW. Hundreds of airplanes, streaming in at high speeds and altitudes from around the nation and world, are funneled and spaced through the narrow gate on his radar screen. At that point, they are handed off to DFW tower for landing clearance.

Dave has been trained to handle distractions of all kinds. Each radar target is a possible collision disaster as airplanes slow from 500 mph to 210 mph. He issues exact speeds, headings, and altitudes to pilots as he triangulates planes from all directions through his initial control and release path. The precise radio commands that he transmits are akin to the words of Jesus in the seventh chapter of Matthew. Pilots take the commands of air traffic controllers very seriously. Imprecise response of a flight crew can produce great danger and chaos in their lives. Narrow is the gate and exact is the heading that leads to life and safe landing.

Dave says Satan only has to get a person or church a few degrees off course to miss the gate. Two or three degrees are all that are needed. Our spiritual directional gyro must be set with the heavenly compass, or we will drift off course. Many will think that just because they have been heading generally in the right direction (we prophesied, cast out demons, and performed miracles in your name) yet too late will hear the words, "I don't know you."

We must take the Word of God seriously. The words of Jesus in Matthew 7 confirm that he does not want us to be just part of a religious stream or movement. He commands us to enter the way at the straight gate if we would be his disciple.

THE FLIGHT OPERATING MANUAL

I HAVE A PILOT FRIEND who once told me that he had real doubts about the Bible. Just to keep the conversation going I asked him, "Okay, which part do you not believe, the Old Testament or the New Testament?" Then I said to him, "You believe your flight operating manual, don't you?" The flight manual has great parallels to the Holy Bible.

- One tells how the world was created and how to live in it. The other tells how an airplane is created and how to fly it.

- Both help in making decisions about flight and life, while at the gate and in the air.

- Both will take us to actions that we would not necessarily choose to do on our own.

- Both are books of authority and action.

Since then, I have thought a lot about it. The flight handbook and the Bible are important in interpretation.

- Both enable us to do what we love to do and what we should do as we sit in the "cockpit of life."

- Both have history.

- Both provide a safety net.

- Neither helps us make excuses to cancel our flight. Indeed, they rescue our flight.

The flight operating manual is diminished if the pilot is not exceedingly familiar with it. There are chapters which give specific answers, and the pilot must know the spirit of the entire book. He cannot depart from its authority. Its word is law.

The flight operating manual brings earth and heaven together and helps the pilot to fly right. When questions arise, the pilot has many resources. He is not flying solo. He is only one radio call away from dispatch operations, which opens a whole gamut of resources.

God's Word is forever settled in heaven.
Let it forever be settled in our hearts!

The Word of God, the Holy Bible, also brings earth and heaven together. We must trust its Word and not devise our own way. History records God's faithfulness to those who have believed his righteousness and lived by its authority. Its Word is law. When questions arise, the Christian has many resources. He is not flying solo. He is only a radio call away from the enabling help of the Holy Spirit.

God's Word is forever settled in heaven. Let it forever be settled in our hearts.

Whatever conflict and disbelief we experience in our life shows a departure from living under the authority of his Word. If we do not keep the Bible current in our thinking, we make it irrelevant and out of date in our lives. However, if we trust God's Word daily, the Scriptures affirm our faith in Jesus Christ, our worship, and our ethics and morals. It empowers us to straighten up and fly right.

MAKING ROOM FOR GOD

WHEN I WAS HIRED AS a flight officer with United Airlines, I was a very experienced pilot with seven thousand hours of flight and an impeccable safety record. I was glad to be one of the "sheep." Little did I know the baptism of fire that I would undergo in my initial training.

The first thing I learned in training was that I would have to become a "walking flight manual" My way of doing flight had to go. Flying the line was far too big and specific to fit the old flow patterns I had learned. I simply could not fit my old habits into the new holy crew concepts. The community of pilots with which I now would be flying are all trained to a flight certified SOP (standard operating procedure). Every certified procedure is set apart in captain's authority and covers all flight contingencies. It would be chaos to fly any other way. What's more, if I did not fly the new way, I could still be a pilot but not a United Airlines pilot.

For example, consider the procedure for takeoff. All extraneous conversation must cease. Standard procedure and verbal callouts allowed are:

- Cleared for takeoff…airspeed is alive

- 80 knots power set, instruments crosschecked

- V1… (go, no go decision speed) V2, (takeoff safety speed) Rotate
- positive climb, gear up (maintain V2 plus 10 knots to 800 feet)

- flaps 5…green light, flaps 2…green light, flaps up, set climb thrust

- Accelerate and climb to 3,000 feet (still no conversation except for talking to air traffic control) 250 knots maximum speed below 10,000 feet

I have described just one of many flight maneuvers all designed to keep you out of trouble—a holy standard. It is not rocket science, but it is a safe way of effective flying in the community of diverse pilots who believe in that standard.

The same is true in our Christian life. We have to become the "walking Word of God". Our way of doing things has to go. We sometimes set out trying to fit God into our lives. However, God is too big to fit into our way of doing things. We simply must begin to fit ourselves into his way of doing things. He is the Captain. His way is the set-apart, holy way. All things "are made new."

We often want God to "come along beside us" and help us with our plans and ambitions. But God has far greater plans for us. We are in his holy hands. It is not rocket science. However, we often resist, hoping God will come along and think our way is better. Trying to make room for God in our lives simply does not work. We are too small, and he is too big. God is holy and specific. Likewise, his plans for us are holy and specific.

> *We are not cookies in a cookie-cutter template. We do not all plop out the same way in our culture.*

Now, do not misunderstand me. I know we are not cookies in a cookie-cutter template. We do not all plop out the same way in our culture. However, we cannot be culture Christians either. We are called to Christian standards, measured by Christ's standards. "It is he that hath made us, and not we ourselves; we are his people, and the sheep of his pasture" (Psalm 100:2-3 KJV).

The hard rock reality is this: God is sovereign. Nevertheless, just like the children of Israel in the Old

Testament, we ignore God's way and make for ourselves our own unholy standard operating procedure. Making room for God did not work then, and it does not work now. God does not just want to fill a void in our lives. He wants to dominate our lives. The gospel chorus says, "God's way is my way, and we are his people. God's way is my way, and we are his people. I'll never turn back from God's way."

THE HOLY SPIRIT

THEY CAN FLY THE SKIES and make a lot of noise, but without ammunition, the United States Air Force is just another expensive and noisy flying club. The pilots learn to fly the plane first before they are baptized into the powerful weaponry, without which they are in danger of being shot out of the sky.

Likewise, without the convicting power of the Holy Spirit in the hearts of her people, the church is just another social works club. Christ's provision saves and forgives us of our sins, but only the baptism of the Holy Spirit can empower us for service. We can have great teaching. We can have powerful and eloquent preaching (and we are thankful). However, without the Holy Spirit invading our hearts and our worship, we are just a flying club of sorts. We can pull the trigger and have no fire power. The Apostle Paul gave this urgent warning to his dear people at Galatia. It had become a noisy powerless church: "You have become estranged from Christ, you who attempt to be justified by law; you have fallen from grace. For we through the Spirit eagerly wait for the hope of righteousness by faith" (Galatians 5:4-5 NJKV).

The benefits of the Holy Spirit in our lives are enormous. We can face uncertainty and lurking danger with confidence and assurance. We are not alone.

Jesus promised his disciples the gift of the Holy Spirit after his death and resurrection. Everything was changed. Without the Holy Spirit at work in our hearts, we become a slave at the hands of our good deeds and are in danger of becoming seedless fruit, as Jesus warned his disciples in John 15:4. We need the Holy Spirit moving among us in worship and convicting power. We must not quench the Holy Spirit. We have to confess our dependence upon God's moving and power, or we fall powerless in an unbelieving culture. We need the ammunition of the Holy Spirit. The baptism of the Spirit empowers us for service. If we claim Christ, we must continue in the Holy Spirit. We cannot serve any other way.

Scripture says, "Repent, and let every one of you be baptized in the name of Jesus Christ for the remission of sins; and you shall receive the gift of the Holy Spirit" (Acts 2:38 NIV). "Put on the full armor of God, so that you will be able to stand firm against the schemes of the devil" (Ephesians 6:11 NIV).

Prayer: Lord, send the reviving favor and fragrance of your Holy Spirit in my life today. Without your Holy Spirit, my mission is powerless.

WHERE WAS THE POWER?

ON JANUARY 17, 2008, AFTER a twelve-hour flight, a British Airways Boeing 777 landed 1,200 feet short of the runway at Heathrow Airport in London. On short final, power was needed to arrest a sink rate that was taking the big plane to a touchdown well short of the touchdown point on the runway. Landing short or long is a possibility that pilots are trained to avoid. According to the flight crew, power was added and the engines did not respond. Where was the power? How could this happen?

As an airline pilot, I refuse to second-guess aircraft accidents. The flight data recorders will certainly yield information about the last several minutes of this flight. Here are some facts that are common to all jet passenger aircraft on final approach to touchdown. All landings require considerable power settings.

1. All final approaches must be stabilized: on target speed, target flight path, landing configuration, checklist complete, and landing power set (spooled up engine rpm)

2. Rate of descent must be less than one thousand feet per minute.

3. Landings with severe weather nearby can include sudden up-and-down drafts.

Any deviation from these parameters is an instant red flag that demands immediate attention. Within five hundred feet of the ground, a go-around procedure is required. So the questions are: Where was the power? At what point was it needed? Did all engines lose thrust during approach?

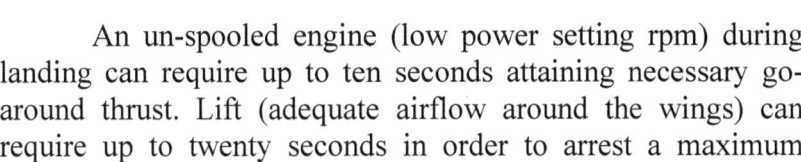

An un-spooled engine (low power setting rpm) during landing can require up to ten seconds attaining necessary go-around thrust. Lift (adequate airflow around the wings) can require up to twenty seconds in order to arrest a maximum allowed rate of descent of one thousand feet.

In mere seconds, a large aircraft on short final can easily lose 150 feet of altitude and land 1,500 feet short of the runway if adequate power is not maintained. This is the reason the engines must be powered up all the way to touchdown. Where was the power? Was it a fuel problem, or was it mismanaged? Was it slow response to a downdraft? Was the flight crew tired or distracted? I think we will know these answers soon.

We need God's power at critical points for spiritual living.

Like an airliner on final approach, we each need God's power at critical points for spiritual living. Making timely decisions within his parameters will keep us safe in unstable times. It is easy to get tired or distracted. Keep your life spooled up in the Word of God. "Who being the brightness of his glory and the express image of his person, uphold all things by the word of his power" (Hebrews 1:3 KJV). "I have fought a good fight, I have finished my course, I have kept the faith" (2 Timothy 4:7 KJV).

CONTAMINATED FUEL

AIRLINE PILOTS PUT A GREAT deal of faith in fuel suppliers and handlers who transport fuel and refuel their airplanes. Contaminated fuel is a scary thought at 35,000 feet and certainly no place or time to wonder about trustworthy fuel.

At high, cold, and hostile altitudes, where airplanes fly best, temperatures often are minus sixty-five degrees below zero centigrade. Jet fuel (kerosene) tends to slowly turn into petroleum jelly on the way to the engines, and ice contaminants form from water moisture and condensate at those extreme temperatures. However, don't stop flying yet.

Engine flameout was a problem at high altitudes on early jet technology, until we learned that cold petroleum jelly does not flow well through fuel supply lines and igniter nozzles. Engine flameout occurred mostly when power was reduced to flight idle during initial descent. With perfectly good fuel in the tanks, fuel was freezing in the fuel lines going to the engine.

Technology invented fuel heat systems, and flameout problems were solved using hot exhaust from each jet engine to warm the fuel lines before descent. A fuel additive (called pristine) disperses water droplets, preventing ice contamination in the wing fuel tanks. We also learned new ways fuel could be refined, removing other foreign impurities.

In short, pilots must always beware of contaminated fuel.

The Word of God is the fuel that propels our Christian lives into truthful and right living. God's Word is refined, warm, and suitable. However, we often contaminate it with our own man-made ideas and additives. God's Spirit and power are quenched when our supply lines are contaminated with foreign matter. Man-made theology creeps in to deceive us and blatantly quenches the Holy Spirit in our lives to know God's truth. Feel good theology is "watered down" from God's pristine standards.

*Contaminated fuel will leave
you empty and flame out.*

Do not believe every word you hear or read. "Contaminated fuel" will leave you empty and flamed out. Also, do not put contaminated fuel in your tanks. Get it straight from the refined Word of God. It is trustworthy.

Prayer: Dear Lord, sometimes we try to stay spiritually airborne with our throttles set at flight idle. Give us new power settings. Let the refining fire of your Word reach our frozen souls so that The Holy Spirit will flow in and through us. Amen.

THE RETURN FLIGHT HOME

FOR ALL WHO TRAVEL, THE return flight home is most welcome! I have often made this announcement over the cabin intercom after landing in Orlando, Florida: "To those who have just begun your visit here, have a great time at Mickey Land. To those who are ending their travel here, welcome home."

But every time I think of those words, I am reminded of the scripture, "For here we have no continuing city, but we seek the one to come" (Hebrews 13:14 NKJV). This world is not our home but only a temporary dwelling place. Like the Apostle Paul told young Timothy, we must stir the spiritual gifts within us as we journey to our eternal destination. Confirming and purposing in our heart, we believe what God is doing. He is setting the world right, joining our future with his present in righteous judgment.

We believe what God is doing.
He is setting the world right.

We can fly to distant world destinations and find temporary happiness. But as the poet said, this world is but a vale of sorrow compared to the eternal joy that awaits us at our final destination. There are no more exciting words than these from the Scripture:

> Behold, I tell you a mystery: We shall not all sleep, but we shall all be changed, in a moment, in the twinkling of an eye, at the sound of the last trumpet. For the trumpet will sound and the dead will be raised incorruptible and we shall be changed. (1 Corinthians 15:51 KJV)

> For we must all appear before the judgment seat of Christ, so that each one may be recompensed for his deeds in the body, according to what he has done, whether good or bad.
> (2 Corinthians 5:10 ESV)

> And just as it is appointed for man to die once, and after that comes judgment (Hebrews 9:27 ESV).

We live in God's sanctity of space where he is employed in the story of our recovery and redemption. He is making us fit for our final dwelling place with him. "There is therefore now no condemnation for those who are in Christ Jesus" (Romans 8:1). God's Holy Spirit is enabling us to eternal rest in heaven. Jesus says, don't look here—look there! Don't just ride along. Follow me! I am your hope. "I go to prepare you a place, that where I am, there you may be also" (John 14:3).

There have been hundreds of times after a long day of flying, when we look out the windshield while in descent, and see the distant glow of our destination. The overcast is behind us . . . the under cast has dissipated and I know that somewhere in that city glow I will rest that night.

Are we there yet? No, but I can see the lights of the city!

"Precious in the sight of the LORD is the death of his saints" (Psalm 116:15).

DON'T WORRY

I BORROW A STORY THAT you might have heard. The author is unknown.

Years ago, I was enthralled as I listened to a pastor as he concluded his message. He told of one of the most frightening yet thought-provoking experiences of his life. He had been on a long flight. The first warning of the approaching problems came when the sign on the airplane flashed on. "Fasten your seat belts a calm voice said, "We will not be serving the beverages at this time, as we are expecting a little turbulence. Please be sure your seat belt is fastened."

As he looked around the aircraft, it became obvious that many of the passengers were becoming apprehensive. Later, the voice of the announcer said, "We are so sorry that we are unable to serve the meal at this time. The turbulence is still ahead of us."

Then we flew into the narrowing passage of the storm cells. The ominous cracks of thunder could be heard even above the roar of the engines. Lightning lit up the darkening skies, and within moments, that great plane was like a cork tossed around on a celestial ocean. One moment the airplane lifted on terrific currents of air; the next, it dropped as if it were about to crash.

The pastor confessed that he shared the discomfort and fear of those around him. He said, "As I looked around the plane, I could see that nearly all the passengers were upset and alarmed. Some were praying. The future seemed ominous, and many were wondering if they would make it through the turbulence.

Then I suddenly saw a little girl. Apparently the turbulence meant nothing to her. She had tucked her feet beneath her as she sat on her seat; she was reading a book, and everything within her small world was calm and orderly.

Sometimes she closed her eyes; then she would read again; then she would straighten her legs, but worry and fear were not in her world. When the plane was being buffeted so badly, when it lurched this way and that, as it rose and fell with frightening severity, when all the adults were scared half to death, that marvelous child was completely composed and unafraid."

The minister could hardly believe his eyes. It was not surprising, therefore, that when the plane finally reached its destination and all the passengers were hurrying to disembark, our pastor lingered to speak to the girl whom he had watched for such a long time. Having commented about the storm and behavior of the plane, he asked why she had not been afraid. The child replied, "'Cause my daddy's the pilot, and he's taking me home."

"Behold, God *is* my salvation, I will trust and not be afraid; For YAH, the LORD, *is* my strength and song; He also has become my salvation" (Isaiah 12:2 NKJV).

DON'T MISS GOD'S GLORY

WE TOOK OFF FROM CHICAGO O'Hare one early afternoon on an October day with 152 passengers. It was a blazing clear day; our destination, Burlington, Vermont. During the cloudless flight we enjoyed a 150 knot tailwind at 35,000 feet approaching the speed of sound across the ground. At 120 miles from our destination, I requested a lower altitude and was cleared to descend to cruise 6,000 feet. ATC was putting our flight plan totally at our discretion, always a fun way to fly.

I pulled the throttles to flight idle and pushed the nose down to keep the speed up. As we rapidly descended out of 14,000 feet, I suddenly realized what an incredible sight was developing out the front windshield below us. The blazing sunlight was reflecting off the forest hills and valleys in vivid autumn colors of bright reds, yellows, and greens.

We slowed to 250 knots and were cleared down to 3,000 feet. At fifteen miles out ATC transmitted, "United 1114, you're number two for the airport, traffic no factor, call tower now, one one-eight point three, good day."

I replied, "United 1114. Thank you, sir, switching now; good day."

As we descended, the view was increasingly growing in wild beauty as sunlight bounced off the autumn-painted forest hills of Lake Champlain. It was overwhelming! I offered the first officer the controls and the landing. He accepted.

I switched to tower frequency and spoke into my microphone, "Burlington tower, United 1114 out of five thousand for three, requesting scenic tour circling approach to a seven-mile final runway one five."

"Roger, United 1114, cleared visual approach. One five as requested, call the marker inbound."

"Roger, we'll call the marker for landing."

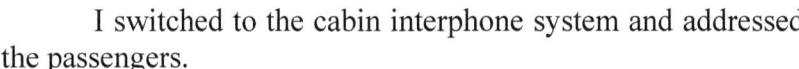

I switched to the cabin interphone system and addressed the passengers.

"Ladies and gentlemen: this is your captain. What a beautiful autumn day here in Burlington! Don't miss God's glory. I wish you all could look out our windshield and see the panoramic view we are enjoying of this glorious place. If you are lucky enough to be sitting by a window, please share this view with your neighbor. Drink it in. It is magnificent.

"We'll be making some turns, so you can enjoy the landscape. If you are visiting this area, take time to get out and see this place. If you are lucky enough to live here, don't take it for granted. It's a beautiful place. Don't miss the glory.

"Flight attendants, prepare for landing."

After we parked at the gate, there was a festoon of smiling faces and many warm exchanges of gratitude from the locals. It was one of the most remarkable deplaning experiences I had ever witnessed. That day, we did not miss God's glory!

"Moses said, 'I pray to you, show me your shining-greatness!' And God said, 'I will have my goodness pass in front of you. I will make the name of the Lord known in front of you'" (Exodus 33:18-19 NLV).

HOLIDAY FLYING

HOLIDAY FLYING CAN BE HECTIC with large crowds in the terminals and gate areas. However, along with the crowded boarding of airplanes, there is excitement that one feels among the passengers as they anticipate the joys of family reunions—children seeing their grandparents and special hours spent together in traditions that go beyond occasional visits.

I sometimes tell passengers upon gate arrival, "Merry Christmas," or "Happy Hanukah." Recently I have added this: "If the holiday does not matter to you, have a truly good day," and "Please come see us again."

Holidays are holy days. We most naturally express our faith on these days. Exercising "faith" is a natural expression for an airline pilot, and the holiest of all days for me is the Easter season. It is what I most fervently believe.

The Christian cross is the power unto salvation.

The glory of the cross is good news.

There is no salvation without the cross.

We celebrate the Easter season because we see the fulfillment of biblical prophesy. "When Jesus had finished saying all these things, he looked up to heaven and said, 'Father, the time has come. Glorify your Son so he can give glory back to you'" (John 17:1 NIV). Jesus was going back to heaven. He was going by way of the cross, shedding his life's blood for the forgiveness of man's sins. "And now, Father, bring me unto the glory we shared before the world was" (John 17:5 NKJV).

The cross of Jesus Christ is the
central theme of the Bible.

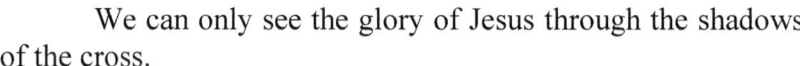

We can only see the glory of Jesus through the shadows of the cross.

It is amazing how eclectic Christianity becomes when the cross is omitted from our teaching and thinking. We live in such a day. Yet Christianity is not eclectic but specific: the virgin birth, the cross, the resurrection and second coming. Without all of these, Christian conversion makes no sense at all.

Advanced eclectic ideas are pervasive in Christian thought today. Nevertheless, God's Word is unchanging. The glory of the cross outshines them all. The crucified and risen Jesus is the cornerstone of our salvation. Diverse Christian opinion becomes pale in the glory of the cross. There is no cross-less Christianity…no Christ-less Christianity. Christian diversity fades in the glory of the cross.

The cross of Jesus Christ is the central theme of the Bible. One can believe a lifetime, but Jesus makes no sense outside his relationship to the cross he bore. Jesus did not die to give us a better life but to redeem our eternal souls. "We are bought with a price."

I have exercised flying faith in the air for over twenty thousand hours. But this is the faith I most fervently believe—faith that guides me through the journey of life to eternal life.

We can "turn over a new leaf," but we are still dead in our sins without the power of the cross of Jesus. It is this Jesus that we must see if we are to behold the salvation of the cross: "Behold the Lamb of God, which takes away the sins of the world" (John 1:29 KJV). We cannot rid ourselves of even the smallest sin any other way. No man can take his glory from him. This is the specific glory of the cross. "O death, where is your sting? Oh grave, where is your victory?" (1 Corinthians 15:55 KJV).

Prayer: Lord, make every day a holiday in your presence and a holy day in your sight. Amen.

BELIEVING IN THE WORD OF GOD

I BELIEVE IN THE LAWS of physics. I have observed these laws trustworthy in my 21,000 hours of flight. In the classroom and in the air, I have interfaced aerodynamic design with the laws of inertia, lift, gravity, thrust and drag and honestly have never been surprised how they work together.

If you've read this book, you know that I believe in the Holy Bible. It is a book of wisdom, instruction and correction. I am thankful to have had the chance to review some of my favorite scriptures as they relate to life, vocation and living.

I believe the Bible in the same way I believe in the laws of physics. Although I cannot fully explain physical laws in scientific terms, I find them dependable and predictable. I believe the Bible in a literal sense of the word. That is, I believe God's Word to be dependable and trustworthy. The answer is yes . . . I have no trouble believing the Word of God, by faith and reason. It is as relevant today as it was in the day that is was first given to us.

Just as we cannot change the laws of physics by debating them, our instructions are to rightly divide the Word of God, not to debate it. Literally or metaphorically, I accept its worth. I'll not make excuses for its social inferences that seem strange for our day. Nor will I tiptoe around its mysteries.

The Word of God and the laws of physics are written by the same Author. We can trust them both by faith or we can break them at our peril. It should be easy to believe the Word of God, handed down to us in miraculous ways that is empirically proven in other documents of history.

The Bible is the books of faith, about a people of faith who are justified by faith amid undeniable prophesy of the risen Messiah. Our inability to explain the mysteries and miracles of the Bible does not make them unbelievable, but rather possible.

I believe the Bible is true, even in the dimensions I cannot see or explain. The Holy Bible is astonishing, discernable and undeniable. It is hidden but yet revealed. It is living but unchanging. It is eternal and unmeasured. It is comforting, yet it cuts to pieces our pretenses.

EPILOGUE

THE STORY

THERE HAVE BEEN MANY ATTEMPTS to destroy the story of God's Word through the ages. Its survival is one of the great marvels, mysteries, and miracles of many centuries. God declares: "Heaven and earth will pass away, but my words will never pass away" (Matthew 24:35 NIV). God is telling us the story in the details of our lives. He puts us in the captain's seat and writes us into the story. We find it is a love story, and we discover him.

It is the greatest story ever told—the story of all Creation—how we came to be and who we are. It is the story of our fall and our redemption. The story ultimately answers every question that we can ask, every answer that we seek, and every solution that we need. The story finds us on the flight deck of our life, on the journey of our life! We get to encounter all of what life is about. We experience the drama, the struggle, the pursuit of all things. We make a few bad landings but have the ultimate chance to find meaning in all of it. However, unable to explain it to ourselves, amid all the evidence, we must believe the story by faith.

I was not paying enough attention when I first heard the story, and I only caught snatches of it. I tried to explain the story, but I could not understand the inexplicable. I tried to deny that there was a story, but I had already heard too much. Every time I turned on the light, I could see more of what was happening, and it made sense to me. It is a story of discovery, and I know it is true. Man did not make it up. Man, in his wildest dreams, could not make it up.

Our story keeps unfolding because the journey is always before us. The story stretches all of time—as far back as we can remember and as far ahead as we can see. God empirically documents the story with earth-shaking events and prophecies. The story is universal and is for all nations. We discover that our journey takes us to our final destination of eternal life. In that great day, we will meet our Maker, the lover of our souls, and our eternal king. Our journey will be over. We will set the parking brake at the final gate. For here, we have no continuing place, but we seek one to come: "For this world is not our permanent home; we are looking forward to a home yet to come" (Hebrews 13:14 NLT).

FINALLY HOME

When engulfed by the terror of tempestuous sea,
Unknown waves before you roll;
At the end of doubt and peril is eternity,
Though fear and conflict seize your soul:

But just think of stepping on shore, and finding it heaven!

Of touching a hand and finding it God's!
Of breathing new air and finding it celestial!
Of waking up in glory and finding it home!

> Words by Don Wyrtzen and L.E. Singer
> Published by Singspiration Music;
> Zondervan Corporation
> Grand Rapids, Michigan

MY ETERNAL KING

My God, I love Thee;
Not because I hope for heaven thereby,
Nor yet because who love Thee not
Must die eternally.

Thou, O my Jesus, Thou didst me upon the cross embrace;
For me didst bear the nails, and manifold disgrace,
Why, then why, O blessed Jesus Christ, Should I not love Thee well?
Not for the hope of winning heaven, Or of escaping hell;

Not with the hope of gaining aught, Not seeking a reward;
But as Thyself has loved me, O ever loving Lord!

Even so I love Thee, and will love
And in Thy praise will sing;
Solely because Thou art my God,
And my Eternal King.

> Poem (anonymous) from 17th Century Latin
> Translated by Rev. Edward Caswall

HIGH FLIGHT

Oh! I have slipped the surly bonds of earth
And danced the skies on laughter-silvered wing;
Sunward I've climbed, and joined the tumbling mirth
Of sun-split clouds—and done a hundred things
You have not dreamed of—wheeled and soared and swung
High in the sunlit—silence. Hov'ring there
I've chased the shouting wind along, and flung
My eager craft through footless halls of air.
Up, up the long delirious, burning blue,
I've topped the windswept heights with easy grace
Where never lark, or even eagle flew
And, while with silent lifting mind I've trod
The high untresspassed sanctity of space,
Put out my hand and touched the face of God.

Pilot Officer Gillespie Magee
No. 412 squadron, RCAF
Killed December 1941

FURTHER INFORMATION

RENDA AUTHORS A BLOG AND weekly morning musings on his website. For further information please visit:

www.RendaWrites.com

or feel free to contact the author by email at:

rendaual@aol.com

For Further Study and Discussion
"Life at 35,000 Feet" can be an open discussion for spiritual perspective.

Here are suggested ideas for group leaders how conversational study groups can participate in open discussion about their vocations and life experiences, using these stories.

Method 1
Considering the dynamics of the meeting room, The **Study Coordinator** divides the attendees into smaller table groups. (five or six in each group works well).
The **Study Coordinator** assigns a story title from the book (page number) for all table groups to read silently and then discuss quietly. (4-8 minutes) Each table names a **Spokesman** that will take notes and represent that table for their discussion. Subsequent open discussion about that story then ensues with all tables: A traveling microphone aids in communication and concise thought during the group discussion.
Study Coordinator keeps the clock and moves the agenda along. He calls the groups back together and divides the remaining time for other assigned stories as time allows.
Each meeting should be an agreed time for about an hour session. (The larger the groups, of course the fewer stories per session) Allow time for comment and closure.

Method 2
Using the total group, the **Study Coordinator** assigns a story or two for all to read.
They then discuss their "takeaways" from the text and how it can relate to vocational matters and decisions. Shorter remarks allow more participation. Wrap up the time with comment and closure.

www.ingramcontent.com/pod-product-compliance
Lightning Source LLC
Chambersburg PA
CBHW071658090426
42738CB00009B/1571